SHANGHAI'S SCHEMOZZLE

SHANGHAI'S SCHEMOZZLE

VOLUMES 1 AND 2 TOGETHER

by Sapajou with
R.T. Peyton-Griffin
("In Parenthesis")

With a Foreword by Richard Rigby

First published in 1937
by the North-China Daily News

Reprinted by
China Economic Review Publishing
Hong Kong 2007

Shanghai's Schemozzle
By Sapajou with R.T. Peyton-Griffin ("In Parenthesis")

With a new foreword by Richard Rigby

ISBN-13: 978-988-17149-5-4

© 2007 Earnshaw Books

Shanghai's Schemozzle was first published in 1937 by the North-China Daily News.

HISTORY / Asia / China

First printing September 2007
Second printing June 2008

EB015

All rights reserved. No part of this book may be reproduced in material form, by any means, whether graphic, electronic, mechanical or other, including photocopying or information storage, in whole or in part. May not be used to prepare other publications without written permission from the publisher except in the case of brief quotations embodied in critical articles or reviews. For information contact info@earnshawbooks.com

Published by Earnshaw Books Ltd. (Hong Kong)

CONTENTS

Foreword by Richard Rigby   7

Shanghai Schemozzle Volume 1   17

Shanghai Schemozzle Volume 2   89

Sapajou and "Shanghai's Schemozzle"
by Richard Rigby

Shanghai's Schemozzle was produced in two parts – the second following the popularity of the first – as a compilation of the cartoons of Sapajou and the text edited and in part written by "In Parenthesis", the pen name of R.T Peyton-Griffin. Peyton-Griffin was the long-term editor of the *North-China Daily News*, the voice par eminence of the largely British establishment of the International Settlement in Shanghai. It was probably the most important and prestigious English language newspaper in the entire Far East (cartoon p.79), and as its editor, Peyton-Griffin ("Peyt" to his colleagues) deserves a biography in his own right.

While the integration of text and cartoons are fundamental to the success of Shanghai's Schemozzle, it is the cartoons that speak most directly to the modern reader – such being the nature of the medium – unlike the text, where diction and attitudes can at times alienate as well as enlighten. But here, too, may reside its greatest value: not for what it tells us of the events themselves, which are well known enough, but for the insight into what Arthur Ransome, writing in a highly critical but perceptive article in 1927, described as "The Shanghai Mind", i.e. the mind of those who made and ran the International Settlement.

Nowhere has the Shanghai and China of which Ransome wrote been better portrayed than in the works of Sapajou, and Shanghai's Schemozzle is the best and most typical compilation of his work currently available in book form.

Sapajou was the artistic nom-de-plume of Georgii Avksent'ievich Sapojnikoff, one-time lieutenant of the Russian Imperial Army. He was a graduate of the Aleksandrovskoe Military School in Moscow, and saw action in World War I, in which he was gravely wounded. As a result of his wounds, which left him with a pronounced limp for the rest of his life, he was invalided out of the army, and it was at this time that he began to take an interest in the visual arts, enrolling in evening classes at the Academy of Arts.

The year 1920 found him, like so many of his compatriots, a refugee in Shanghai. He joined the *North-China Daily News* in 1925, and through his daily cartoons, published over an almost unbroken period of fifteen years, became well known not only in Shanghai but also internationally. The publishing house of Kelly & Walsh produced several albums of his sketches of Shanghai life, and his illustrations appeared in a number of contemporary books on Chinese subjects. He was also Director and shareholder of the Shanghai Russian publishing house and newspaper Slovo.

Sapajou had the relatively rare distinction for a White Russian of being a member of the exclusive Shanghai Club, famed for its long bar – allegedly the longest in the world (cartoons pp.59,67) – and also of the Cercle Sportif Francais, the premises of which now form part of the Garden Hotel. He was tall, bespectacled and distinguished in appearance. A Russian lady of my acquaintance who knew him at the height of his popularity recalled that "all the girls loved him". He walked with a cane as a result of his war wound.

Following Japan's declaration of war on Britain and the United States in December 1941 and their occupation of the International Concession, Sapajou had to seek work elsewhere. For a professional cartoonist and stateless person – hence not subject to the internment that was the lot of most of his colleagues who had been unable to escape the Japanese – the choices were few, and in order not to starve he joined

the local German newspaper, which was of course controlled by the Nazis.

Peyton-Griffin, on the other hand, was quickly arrested and taken by the Kempetai to their notorious torture centre at the Bridge House, on the Hongkou side of the Suzhou Creek. After the Kempetai had finished with him he was offered repatriation, but refused it as this would have meant leaving behind the Russian woman with whom he lived, so he was interned in the relatively milder conditions of the Ash Camp on the Great Western Road (Hongqiao Lu) and reemerged in late 1945 to edit the first post-war (and soon after the 1949 communist takeover of the city the last) edition of the *North-China Daily News*.

For Sapajou, however, after the war things could not be the same. While many of his former colleagues were sympathetic to his predicament, such were the times and the situation that it was not possible for him to return to his former job. The next few years were difficult ones for him, and eventually, shortly before the Communist takeover, he was evacuated by UNWRA with many other White Russians, refugees twice over, to a displaced persons camp on the island of Tubabao in the Philippines. Already seriously ill, he died not long after arrival.

Such a sad ending to a life lived through turbulent times can not, alas, be seen as in anyway atypical for a man of Sapajou's background and period. What does mark him out from the crowd is the remarkable body of work he left behind, a fascinating, indeed brilliant, record of a vanished world, which taken in toto is a still insufficiently appreciated resource for students and scholars alike, and which can also provide great enjoyment to anyone with an interest in China in general or Shanghai in particular, especially at a time when that great city is drawing on its native and exotic genius to recreate itself after half a century of denial. It is to be hoped that the republication of Shanghai Schemozzle may mark the beginnings of a rediscovery of Sapajou's work, and it is very much to the credit of the publishers that they recognize its value.

* * *

Ever since Japan defeated China in 1896, taking Taiwan as part of the spoils of war, it had been closely involved in Chinese affairs, generally negatively, and as opportunity presented itself, continued to nibble away at Chinese territory — Manchuria, Jehol (roughly corresponding to northern Hebei), Inner Mongolia — a process marked by intermittent hostilities, including savage clashes in Shanghai in 1932. By 1937 it was ready to launch a full-scale war, which began in March with the Marco Polo Bridge incident just outside Beijing (then Peiping, the national capital being Nanjing).

The first shots of the battle to gain Shanghai were fired on August 9. Two and a half months of fierce fighting ensued as the Japanese engaged some of Chiang Kai-shek's best divisions and strong popular resistance. Japanese war-ships in the Huangpu river shelled the Chinese city remorselessly, and Japanese aircraft conducted a programme of bombing of civilian areas – in those days still something of a novelty (cartoon p.87). Between August and November, when Chinese defenses crumbled, three square miles of the city were destroyed, and much of its environs devastated; nearly a quarter of a million Chinese were killed, including many women and children; and the Japanese military itself lost over 9,000 dead and 31,000 wounded. Japan's victory in Shanghai opened the way for the advance on Nanjing (cartoon p.153), with the horrific and tragic consequences that continue to dog relations between China and Japan to this day.

While these events unfolded, the inhabitants of the International Settlement of Shanghai had a ringside seat, albeit at times an uncomfortably close one (cartoon p.39), and it is this stage of the Sino-Japanese War of 1937-1945 that Shanghai Schemozzle covers. It deals principally with the effect of the hostilities on the Settlement itself, and is very much a work by Shanghailanders – as they liked to refer to themselves – for Shanghailanders. As such, it provides invaluable insights into the attitudes and experiences of this very special group of people, unique in time and place. Perhaps even more importantly, it shows us the International Settlement itself at a time when, even if they did not know it, the privileged existence of those who ran it was coming to an end, and a time when some people at least, under the pressure of external events, were beginning to query at least a few of the propositions that had appeared basic to the Shanghailanders' way of viewing things.

One of the things that had been changing was the attitude to Japan. Many Westerners in China had given grudging, and sometimes more than grudging, admiration to Japan, not least for its "no nonsense" attitude towards Chinese agitation for the recovery of full sovereignty. It was seen as a force for the sort of stability that served the interests of the foreigners in the Treaty Ports, especially Shanghai. However, a divergence of interests became apparent as Japan strengthened its position in North East China, and from time of the 1932 hostilities one can see the beginnings of a more sympathetic attitude towards China. As the decade advanced, the lines were step-by-step more clearly drawn, as Japan was seen increasingly as threat rather than a contributor to the status quo that served Shanghai interests so well (cartoon p.55).

Moreover, the sufferings of ordinary Chinese during the 1937 fighting were such that even the most hardened denizens of the Shanghai Club could not be entirely oblivious (cartoons pp.53,83), and sympathetic individuals and charities did what they could to alleviate civilian suffering – for example the non-combatant safe zone, negotiated with the Chinese and Japanese authorities by the French priest Fr. Jacquinot (cartoon p.133).

More typical of Shanghailander attitudes, though, are the many cartoons on the theme "a plague on both your houses", the most striking of which has an inmate of the Shanghai Lunatic Asylum inviting the combatants to join him inside (cartoon p.99). The war is presented variously as entertainment, a damn nuisance, and a threat to business, and this latter point is without a doubt that which registered most deeply, because it was after all the reason why the overwhelming majority of Shanghailanders were there in the first place (cartoon p.77). It could also, though, be dangerous, despite the Settlement's neutrality, even though such dangers are generally laughed off as minor inconveniences (cartoons pp.73,129,135).

Resilience and good humour under adversity are the persistent themes, supported by a good deal of drinking (cartoons pp.37,59,

69,161).

Behind the bravado, though, there we see a growing sense that things were changing in unpredictable and uncontrollable ways (cartoon p.139). One indication of a changing dispensation was that the China with which the Shanghailanders would henceforth have to deal was no longer one dominated by Western interests, but by Japan (cartoon p.151).

While the general hope was that despite this, life in the concessions would settle back to normal (cartoon p.158), there is a persisting and prescient edginess to both cartoons and text in the latter part of the volume (e.g. cartoon p.161). Writing in the introduction to the second volume, Sapajou and In Parenthesis express the hope "that if Shanghai never has another schemozzle it will, even then, be much too soon". That hope was not to be realized. The world which is so brilliantly captured in Shanghai's Schemozzle came to an end almost exactly four years later.

Richard Rigby was Australian Consul-General in Shanghai (1994-98) and has written widely on Shanghai history

Volume 1

SHANGHAI'S SCHEMOZZLE

by

SAPAJOU

with

R. T. PEYTON-GRIFFIN

("In Parenthesis")

Reprinted from Cartoons and " In Parenthesis " which have appeared in the North-China Daily News between August 11 and September 27, 1937

SHANGHAI
PRINTED AT THE OFFICE OF THE NORTH-CHINA DAILY NEWS & HERALD, LTD
1937

The Genesis of a Joke

A number of readers of the "North-China Daily News" has asked, how it is possible for Sapajou to produce a cartoon regularly, and however he comes to think of the subjects.

It would never do to give trade secrets away .. or at least all of them, .. but this one may be mentioned. At the mention of the word "cartoon," Sapajou sits, looking far away into the distance and meditates. Suddenly he makes a stabbing motion in the air with his pen. An idea has been speared for treatment. Hence a cartoon.

In Parenthesis works entirely differently. He also sits and thinks. It comes more difficult for him .. the thinking we mean.

Then he starts to laugh about nothing in particular, when, suddenly, he grabs hold of himself and mutters:—" 'Ere. Wot are you alaughin' at?"

Directly he finds that out, a joke is born.

Knock! Knock!
Who's There?
Japanese!
Japanese What?
Japan—Is—Friendly!

"SAPAJOU" & "IN PARENTHESIS" OBSERVE THE WAR

From the Military Handbook

There is only one way to catch an aeroplane faster than your own; and that is to put salt on its tail.

* * *

From the Horse's Mouth

In Parenthesis has it on the best possible authority that both sides now have command of the air.

* * *

So Now You Know

"The enemy aircraft were beaten off," extract from communiqué

You can always tell when the enemy aeroplanes are beaten off. They don't stay when they reach their objective.

* * *

Stocked Up

Solicitous Friend.—And how are you off for food?

Old Soak.—Food? Whass tha'?

S.F.:—You know,—Nourishment.

O.S.:—I'm all ri' me boy. I've laid in a case o' gin.

* * *

Notification

In view of the fact that they are in the direct line of fire, In Parenthesis has decided to move his angel fish. When spoken to on the subject they murmured.—" What the hell! "

* * *

From the Front

Old Clubman, watching the evacuees registering.—Looks as if we are becoming quite a social club, doesn't it?

Confirmed Bachelor.—Merely another one of the horrors of war.

Crusty journalist, endeavouring to write something while a lot of gunpowder is being burned outside.—Boy go out and stop that noise.

Boy.—My no b'long Chiang Kai-shih.

Bored businessman watching the bombardment of Pootung.—I wish they'd stop. They'll be hitting something if they're not careful.

What did General Sherman say?

There's been a shortage of ice in the Clubs these last few days.

Sweet Young Thing.—Darling, is this what the common people call war?

Diplomat, and we have several.—Yaas, darling, I believe it is.

Sweet Young Thing.—Well, all I can say is that it is much too dreadful for them.

* * *

A Pending Apology

From the man who called the Armoured Car Company the tinned beef squad.

* * *

An Old Song

"I know a bank whereon the wild thyme grows." Sounds like the Whangpoo, doesn't it?

* * *

The Man We Like

Is the local politician who when the authorities do something to displease him, just takes out his false teeth and lays them on the table to watch them gnash.

* * *

The War Game

Combatant of a certain nation, having crossed no man's land, to a combatant of another certain nation.—" You must take me, or otherwise you will be huffed."

* * *

Another Hard Blow

Owing to the shortage of barbers the men of the city will soon be patronizing the beauty parlours. Permanents will, of course, be the rage, but facials will be administered such as starching the upper lip, if and when necessary.

* * *

Back to Nature!

Foreign Office spokesman . . . . was ordered to leave Nanking immediately, though this was not to be construed as indicating a possible break in the diplomatic relations between China and Japan.

It should be placed on record that the two countries are behaving like two small boys, who, charging each other with their shoulders, mutually exclaim.—' Ere, who're you a'shovin'?

* * *

At the Telephone

Female voice.—Is that the editor of the " North-China Daily News."

A tired Sub-editor.—Yes.

Female voice.—I'm so sorry to bother you. I know you must be busy with all this war and all that, but could you possibly tell me the last film in which John Barrymore played?

"SAPAJOU" & "IN PARENTHESIS" OBSERVE THE WAR

POLITICAL SCIENCE

"SAPAJOU" & "IN PARENTHESIS" OBSERVE THE WAR

Male sozzle a few minutes later.—Is that the "Norsh Shina Daily Newsh"?

Tired Sub-editor, as before.—Yes, what can I do for you?

Male Sozzle.—Well jush settle bet fer ush, will you? Ish it three partsh or three dropsh of angosh—angoshtura for a gin 'nd bittersh?

* * *

On the Best of Authority

Two Japanese divisions have landed at Liuho.

Two Japanese divisions haven't landed at Liuho.

After successfully bombarding Chapoo the Japanese have landed ten divisions and are making towards Shanghai by forced marches.

They aren't!

The fall of Mokanshan is expected any moment.

It isn't!

As the result of a wide encircling movement the enemy are exactly where they started from.

From the progress which both sides are making it is expected that they will shortly have passed completely through each other's lines and be facing back to back.

* * *

A little Psalmody

Spasm I

The guns are popping as they used to pop:
   Who's that a' shootin'?
The bombs are dropping as they used to drop:
   Who's that a' shootin' so spry?
The cops are copping as they used to cop.
   Hurray, we're sayin'
And shoppers are shopping, as they used to shop
   But who's that a' squeezin' so sly?
Who's that a' squeezin'? Who's that a' squeezin'?
   Compradore's are on the make.
Who's profiteering? Who's profiteering.
   Making our bank balance ache?

Spasm II

Way down upon the Whangpoo River
   Boom, boom, they go.
See all the little gunboats shootin'
   Scores of 'em, all in a row
Night comes, and Shanghai's very weary
   Folks home at ten,
Please listen to the pom-poms, dearie,
   Just like the old times agen.
Cabarets are early closing;
   Some clubs shut near nine.
Grass widowers are gently dozing,
   Dreaming of old times so fine.

Notice

The "North-China Daily News" contrary to all rumours is not moving back to the Bund. It never left!

* * *

Big Hearted Bennies

There are still some people keen on admitting all the refugees who apply into the International Settlement. Well, of course, there's nothing like hospitality, is there?

* * *

A Protest

"Portugal has severed diplomatic relations with Czechoslovakia."—News Despatch.

China and Japan, of course, will never do anything so crude.

* * *

How True!

A local contemporary opines:—

   Our recent surmise that major hostilities were at an end may or may not have had basis. . . .

That's just the trouble we have had with our surmises too. They have always been either right or wrong.

* * *

Just a Hint

A hint to the Council, on reading some of the reports issued for local consumption, comes from Dryden:—

   "Now strike the golden lyre again."

Or judging from some of the casualty reports:—

   "And thrice he routed all his foes, and thrice he slew the slain."

* * *

To-day's Great Thought

Something has got to be done about this war. A faithful reader of In Parenthesis, who has been a devout follower of the column, man and boy for the last fifty years, complains of the irregularity of the firing. The other night he dropped off to sleep lulled by the "chant monotonous and deep," of the heavy artillery. He awoke with a start. The firing had stopped, and he fancied he had been plunged into a horrid peace again.

* * *

The Evacuation

A fond mother with young baby at the Shanghai Club on evacuation day. It was imperative that baby should be fed. The paraphernalia was packed away. What to do?

FIGHTING THE FLOOD

"SAPAJOU" & "IN PARENTHESIS" OBSERVE THE WAR

Was there a soul dismayed? Nary one bit. One club man hurried to the chemist and procured the necessary bottle and the mixture which babies, so we are informed, relish and on returning to the Club hot water was secured and the concoction fixed in a *beer mug at the bar*. We do hope it's a boy baby, that lad's had a good start in life.

* * *

Notes on the Crisis

Both sides have still command of the air. If you don't believe us ask them yourselves.

A countryman entering the French Concession on Tuesday with two paniers of canards for sale was set upon by toughs and robbed of them. The police intervened, rescued the canards and arrested some of the robbers.—These "bunders," of course, are feathered.

Things were so quiet round the "N.C.D.N." office yesterday that In Parenthesis is thinking of bringing in a pneumatic drill to make the place seem more homelike.

* * *

Casabianca

BY A LONG-WAY-TO, TIPPERARY-FELLOW

As shot and shell were falling fast,
　A youth climbed up the Race Course mast,
And, gazing round, with a fearful yell,
　He murmured " Casabianca."
Come down at once the Council said.
　He answered swiftly " Boil your head.
You come up here with me instead,
　And holler ' Casabianca.' "
" But what's the scheme ? " the sailor roared
　" I'd teach you better were you on board."
The youth replied in all his pride :
　" By gum, I'd need a thicker hide,
　　　　　　Casabianca."
" Oh, stay ! Oh, stay ! " The soldier cried
　" Until a shot at you I've tried,"
He quickly answered with a laugh
　" I guess you'd hit me. No ? Not 'arf !
　　　　　　Casabianca."
" Just come down here, you poor, dumb mutt."
　She loudly whispered to her lover, but
He looked at her with his sly grin :
　" If I did so, dear, t'would be a sin.
　　　　　　Casabianca."
There oft at curfew he may be seen
　Far above the grassy sward, green,
And from the skies at intervals
　A tender glance so sweetly falls
　　On his sweet girl,
　　His heart's a'whirl,
　Poor Casabianca.
　　For his war girl.

Do You Know?

An American owned concern will supply doughnuts and coffee from six in the morning until ten at night.

British customers are provided with implements to pull the hole out of the doughnut.—Corkscrews are supplied.

* * *

Barber Shortage

Situations Vacant
Wanted.—One Delilah, to cut hair only.

* * *

Classified Ad. Again

Wanted.
One bar of Monkey Brand.

You see we've just been warned we've got to keep this feature clean.

* * *

Another Riddle

Why is a Chinese aviator looking at the Idzumo like the advertisement for a certain brand of toilet soap?

Well, he won't be happy till he gets it.
(N.B. Will the local agents please send the case to . . . .
　Ed. :—Now, now, now . . . .
　I.P. :—Well, if I can't eat I ought to be allowed to wash !)

* * *

From a Communique

Chinese trench mortars situated in the vicinity of the North Station, dropped several shells in the Hongkew area during Thursday night. They, however, ceased firing at dawn according to the communiqué. This was apparently to prevent them from being spotted by the Japanese air force.

The deduction, my dear Watson is obvious.

* * *

Conversation Bromide

"And when do you think all this will end?"

* * *

Agony

Has anyone an electric pot?
No! No! No! We merely want it for one of our linotype machines.

* * *

The Latest Retort

As the Japanese commander said to the Chinese commander: "Don't be so offensive."

THE YOKE THAT FAILED

We're All Coo-Coo

The advent of reinforcements for the international defence force is heartily to be welcomed by some people.—It does make it so much safer to indulge in anti-foreign propaganda, doesn't it?

* * *

Good News

The Japanese, however, through the helpful attitude and active co-operation of the British authorities, are permitting the Brewery to operate normally, *and deliveries are being made.*

War has her victories no less renowned than peace.

* * *

Stop Press

On Thursday a lorry was seen sporting the flag of a certain country,—wild horses won't obtain a further identification—with the bonnet and the roof of the driving seat covered with greenery—If it had only seen itself in the looking glass it would have realized that it did not look like Jessfield Park.

* * *

An Open Letter

The attention of the commanders of the opposing forces is drawn to the growing practice of running aeroplane bombing expeditions just about breakfast time, and it is earnestly requested that some other hour should be selected. It is most distressing. Only the other morning we spilled some hot coffee from the saucer.

* * *

The Optimist

From a local contemporary :—

> Going on the principle of being always thankful for small mercies, residents of this harassed city should derive increasing solace from the established fact that as far as possible, this cosmopolitan area is slowly returning to normalcy

It may be returning to normalcy as far as possible but we, for one, would much prefer it to return a little further.

* * *

It's a bit 'ard

Coming down a side street to the Bund the other morning, we were stopped by a bloke in a tin hat.

"I should not go on the Bund, if I could help it," he said. "If you do so now, it is at your own risk."

"At my own risk?" we replied. "Why all my life I've been living at my own risk. I'm a journalist."

"You're a what? A journalist? *My gawd!*"

And there was not even a blade of grass we could crawl under to hide our shame.

* * *

Answers to Correspondents

Expert.—There is no better 'ole. Scientists are engaged in inventing one which, upon entering, it will be possible to pull in after one.

Enquirer.—Yes, you can tell the different aeroplanes by the sound they make, but we wouldn't liken any of them to humming birds. As a matter of fact we don't like them at all.

A Stay-Behind.—Yes, it is said that if you hear the gun fired the bullet hasn't hit you. But who wants to hang round listening to guns firing?

Dog Lover.—The only thing to distract the dog's attention from the noise is a funny story. If the animal gives you the horse laugh, it is obviously not a dog.

Veteran.—It was a very raw recruit who was found polishing his tin hat!

* * *

Tail-Piece

> TRAMS and buses are again on the streets.—
> News item.

The Bus and the Tram were talking one day,
  As bullets were flying so fast :—
" We've carried and hauled for many a mile
  And nailed the old flag to the mast."
The Bus and the Tram are not like the clam,
  Have many a story to tell,—
Tram drivers who tear through the streets mighty fast,
  Alarms bravely clanging like,—well!
Said the Bus to the Tram, " I don't give a damn.
  In peacetime the people go mad,
With letters to Ed, from brains just like jam,
  To say that my black smoke is bad,
But now that the bullets are flying, and shell,
  I think that we'll both take a rest.
Lay off, do a mike! Let the brutes push a bike!
  We'll stay in the yard with the blest."
Yet fortune orders a different fate.
  They're back on the roads, deep we choke.
The Tram is clanging its bell like—(as before).
  The Bus? It continues to smoke.

"SAPAJOU" & "IN PARENTHESIS" OBSERVE THE WAR

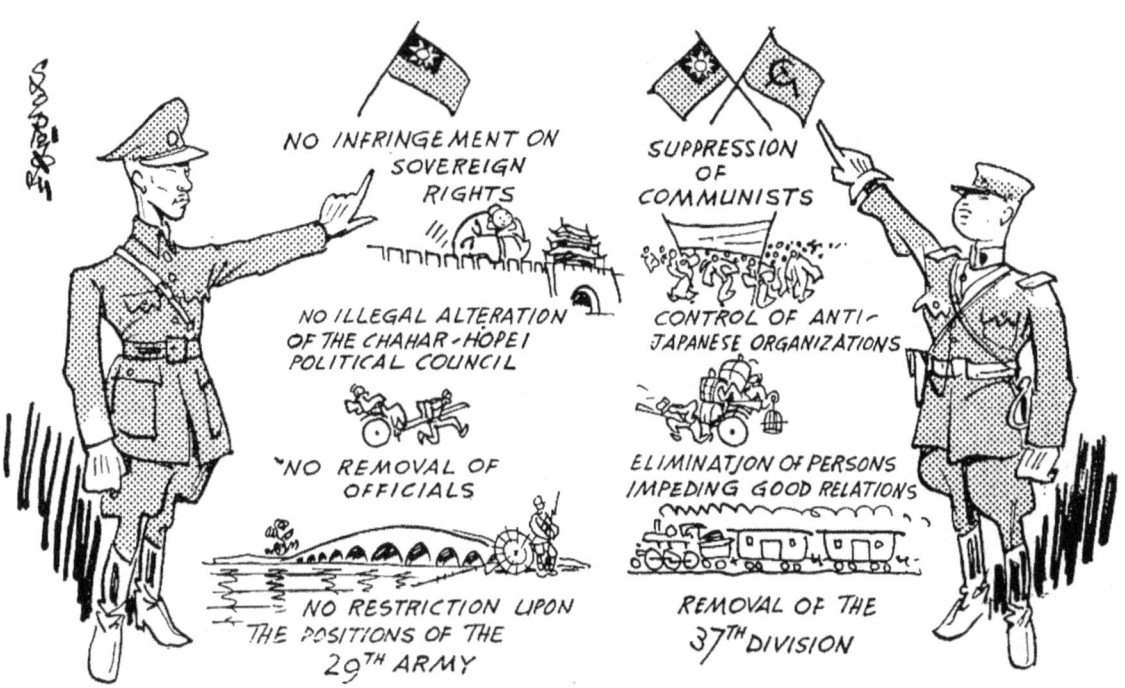

POINTS OF DIFFERENCE

DR. KUNG'S EXCESS LUGGAGE

"SAPAJOU" & "IN PARENTHESIS" OBSERVE THE WAR

Oi!
Did you see that "Positions Vacant" advertisement in the paper the other day?

> Wanted, intelligent, perfect Lady-steno-typist. Address Box . . . . N.C.D.N.

It *is* possible to get an intelligent lady-steno-typist. We saw one once. But if the advertiser is looking for one of those wonderful creatures which are jewelled in every movement, with compensated balance wheel, and all that, we hope he has to wait a very long time, for *perfect* lady-steno-typists are only found in heaven.

* * *

What is it?
Reading the advertisements which appear daily it is quite difficult to ascertain what is going on.

The Municipal Council calls it an emergency.

Another advertiser refers to "present political and financial conditions."

Shipping companies are divided into two schools. One the neorealistic, if you get what we mean, call it "present hostilities."

The other the "present situation."

The advertising department of the N.C.D.N. likes the "Present emergency."

The surrealists prefer "Existing conditions" as best describing the matter.

Yet there are others who want to call it an "incident."

In Parenthesis has been carefully into the matter and has decided that after all it is only a "schemozzle." It stands all tests. Thus:—

S—for shell.
C—for crikey!
H—for hell.
E—for evacuation.
M—mizzle (from Old French v. *mizzler, mizzlé, mizzlant*, to mizzle off as in evacuation).
O—Officers, commanding, or otherwise, who specialize in schemozzles.
Z—for zoophyte, meaning, of course a scrap in a bear garden.
Z—Zephyr, a gentle breeze, from which is derived the phrase "Wind vertical."
L—see H.
E—for 'Eaven.—Thus 'Eaven only knows when it is going to stop.

To Bar Tenders
No one knows what is likely to happen in a schemozzle like this. So take advice. If a gent comes in and leaning over the counter says "Give me a zythum," don't get disturbed and call the bouncer, Give him a glass of beer and a piece of bread.

> Zythum is a liquor made from wheat and malt.

You could, of course boil the bread in the beer, but if you did even the bouncer might not be able to protect you. You can't do that there 'ere when we've got a schemozzle on.

* * *

A Reflection
You know Z is a beautiful letter. Just think. It comes right at the extreme end of the alphabet, and there's not another letter to learn after it. And not only that, it is so expressive as this little story will show.

A Zany and an educated Zulu went into a zygon (A connecting bar; you know, connecting two ends of the room).

Says the Zany to the Zulu.—Wattle?

Says the Zulu to the Zany.—Really, I beg your pawdon.

Zany:—Granted ol' cock! I was merely asking whether you'd care to guzzle the product of a zumological process in which zymes produce a zymotic beverage.

Zulu.—You mean will I accept zome zlight refrezhment?

Zany.—You've got me.

Zulu.—The anzwer iz yez.

Whereupon the Zany reaching for his zax hit the Zulu in the zygomatic region and remarked.—"Iz zat zo?"

(*Printer's Devil*: "—*My gawd! and to think he gets paid fer doing that.*")

* * *

Sporting Notes
In Parenthesis claims to hold the record for sprinting along the Bund. Unofficially, because there was no one to time him, the other morning he did it in 5.2/5 sec., flat.

With a gun from the Idzumo, I.P. made an excellent start. Passing the Custom House, going strong, he continued his pace until just about Canton Road where he put on a terrific spurt reaching the tape . . . . er . . . . we mean the Bar, in the time mentioned.

He was just putting one back, when his shadow, which started level with him but was hopelessly left behind, arrived out of breath.

"SAPAJOU" & "IN PARENTHESIS" OBSERVE THE WAR

THE "WAR" DOGS

LOCALIZING THE BEAST

"SAPAJOU" & "IN PARENTHESIS" OBSERVE THE WAR

Interviewed by the N.C.D.N. In Parenthesis admitted to being a little out of training, but anticipated that by the time the present state of affairs has decided whether it is an emergency or not, he will have reduced his time by about five seconds.

* * *

Grief

A newspaper heading :—
JAPANESE OFFICIAL PESSIMISTIC
Just to think that, in the best and brightest of all beautiful worlds, anyone could be sad.

* * *

Apiculture

And another caption :—
AEROPLANES ENGAGE IN MID-AIR
Any bee-keeper can tell you what happened then.

* * *

A River Happening

They all sank down, and went *boom!*

* * *

Warning

The next person who mentions anything about Nero and his violin when he sees a fire in Chapei will get it where the chicken got the axe.

* * *

War Reporting

A "——" observer who spent the afternoon in the Woosung area, confirmed the landing of troops from six transports but saw no other troop vessel in the area.

A spokesman of the Nanking-Shanghai Garrison Headquarters, at a press conference yesterday afternoon denied the reports that Japanese succeeded in landing troops in the vicinity of Woosung.

In PARENTHESIS assures his readers that there is every chance of one or other of these two consecutive paragraphs in a local contemporary being correct.

* * *

We Broadcast

Hello! Hello! Hello! "This broadcast comes to you through the courtesy of the "North-China Daily News." Here we are in the ringside seats of the biggest prize fight the sporting world has ever seen. Three million people, three million people, folks, are present to-night to see the championship of the Orient decided between two well known heavy-weights. We know there are three million people present, folks, because a million and a half got in without paying. Oh boy! Oh boy! Oh boy! What a crowd! All the best people in Shanghai are here. We have amongst us to-night. . . . who's that white haired gink over there, Mike?

"Aw! cut 'im out."

"All right! all right! all right! Folks I'm here to tell you, this is the biggest fight ever witnessed in the Ori. . . . the Far East I mean. Here he comes, the Tokyo Tiger, weight 4 tsubo, 3 ri, 6 koku. Closely following him into his own corner is the Ding-hao Dandy, from Nanking, weight 8 mow, 3 fung, 1 li and 5 hao. And, boy, how?

"Now the referee is talking to them in the ring. They each return to their corners, and judging from the way they walk, folks, it might be anybody's fight. They didn't shake hands and oh boy, this must be a grudge fight. Both men are trained to the last minute and the confidence of the public in their abilities is such that both are favourites with the big money at evens. There goes the gong for the first round. I will now hand the mike over to Ip! of the 'North-China Daily News.' Here you are Ip."

Ip.—"Hello! hello! hello! This broadcast comes to you through the courtesy of the 'North. . . .'"

The other bloke.—"Aw, can it."

Ip.—"Both men are advancing from their corners looking each other over carefully, and folks what looks, what looks! Now they are feeling each other out, and I hope to tell you, what feeling, what feeling! The Tokyo Tiger leads with his right. . . . no, left, I mean, the Ding-hao Dandy countering with a blow to the jaw and the Tiger goes down for. . . . Sorry folks, my mistake, it's only the referee who has dropped his cigar. Now they are in the middle of the ring looking each other over again, and neither is enjoying the sight. Ding-hao Dandy leads off with a right to the chin, then another right, and another right. They all miss and Tokyo Tiger recovering from the rain of blows steps in and tries for Ding-hao's body. And it's one-two-three, one-two-three, one-two-three! Ding-hao counters with a left-right, left-right, left-right. Oh boy! What a fight! What a fight! Ding-hao steps quickly into the middle of the ring: the Tokyo Tiger quickly follows and if either of them hits the other they'll know all about it. Now they're swapping punches, but they don't hurt each other much. There they go again one-two-three, one-two-three, left-right, left right. Ding-hao Dandy goes down for a one. . . . No, he didn't go down. He

"SAPAJOU" & "IN PARENTHESIS" OBSERVE THE WAR

THE SHANGHAI MELODY OF 1937

"SAPAJOU" & "IN PARENTHESIS" OBSERVE THE WAR

only slipped a little and the gong goes for the end of Round One. I will now hand the microphone over to Horrible Herbert who will sum up the round for you."

Horrible Herbert.—"Hello! Hello! hello! This broadcast comes to you through the courtesy of the 'North.' . . . Sorry! Well folks, what a fight, what a fight! At first I thought it was anybody's fight, but now that I have seen them both in the ring I figger that both of them are going to win. This round has been devoted to looking each other over and feeling each other out, and now that they know what each looks like and how he feels, we may get some action in the next few rounds. But, boys, this round has been full of fight. Ding-hao has been throwing everything except the kitchen stove and the Tokyo Tiger has been replying with the same sort of hardware. I've asked Joe and he says the boys are in the pink. There is no doubt about it, folks: if they both last out they will stay the distance. WHAT A FIGHT, WHAT A FIGHT! We will now take you over to the Santa Lucia Ballroom until the gong sounds for Round Two. It was anybody's round, both the men leading on points, with a shade in favour of each of them.

(*Instructions to printer.—Please set above fifteen times, round by round. I've got something else to do besides type out all this tripe.*

Printer.— *Ses you!*)

* * *

Stop Press!

> Nanking, August 21.—Chinese military information reveals that around 30 Japanese warships have arrived off Pailung Harbour, south of Shanghai along the Chekiang Coast.
>
> Japanese troops reinforcements aboard said vessels, it was stated, were waiting for a chance to land.—"Central News."

It is far from us to question the accuracy of the above report, but isn't it just possible that the men have merely been taken out for a day's fishing?

* * *

Help

Things are going from bad to worse in local journalism, and it is feared that present stresses are warping some people's outlook on life. Take the following for instance :—

> . . . . the cricket season is nearing its end and unless the homeside authorities grant an extension, the football season must start. In this case the pilot who led the expedition is sending up a couple of footballs so that British sporting season procedure should be properly observed, with the proviso that no football pools should be conducted. *These are wicked.*

It is precisely that sort of statement which brings British journalism into disrepute. Football pools are not wicked: we won one once.

* * *

Another Protest

JAPANESE MOONLIGHT RAID ON CHINESE AIRPORT

This is the sort of thing which gets people's backs up. What we mean to say is that, well after all, fair's fair, and unless trade union rules are closely adhered to, how are the enemy to get time off for a spot of sleep?

* * *

Us and the Stenog.

YUNNAN CHAIRMAN OFF FOR KUNMING

I.P.—There ought to be something funny in that. Miss Ipplethwick, will you please give me Joke File No. 13?

Miss Ipplethwick.—That's all about mothers-in-law, Mr. I. P. (*Note she always calls me Mr.*)

I.P.—All right. Put it away. No jokes now about mothers-in-law. It's only in times like this that we realize the good work they do. They harden us for war.

* * *

This War

The reporters of a local contemporary are getting so used to being under fire along the defense lines and in Hongkew and Yangtzepoo that they don't bother to look up any more when planes come over, and they are even getting blasé about snipers. "The editors and rewrite men in the office, however, have escaped being under fire until last night. It was then that two spent machine-gun bullets came through the window near the photographer's dark room . . . . "

When it comes to comparing notes on the schemozzle this newspaper will be able to claim missiles that flew through the composing room from the bomb which struck the Palace Hotel, shrapnel through two windows in the editorial offices, while a delivery coolie in the alleyway at the side of the building got a shot in the pants. But never mind, we are getting our afternoon tea, and the staff takes turns to duck below the only tin hat we have in the office. It's our turn to-morrow!

"SAPAJOU" & "IN PARENTHESIS" OBSERVE THE WAR

COLD COMFORT FOR HOTHEADS

"SAPAJOU" & "IN PARENTHESIS" OBSERVE THE WAR

Scene in Kiukiang Road

Gentleman riding in a rickshaw, pied, canned, sozzled and inebriated, encouraging his puller:—

"Itsh all ri' m'boy. Don' be afraid'. I'm behind 'yer, 'nd the 'ole. . . . . . . navy'sh behin' me. Sho carry on."

* * *

Demonstration

It was only on Monday that we recorded a little passage with a patrol who wouldn't believe we were a newspaperman—pity someone doesn't mistake us for a banker,—and that very day we had a run in with another.

Dropping into the office along Kiukiang Road in our rickshaw, just to see how this war was getting along, we were stopped by a youth wearing a tin hat.

"You can't go down there," he said looking at us as sternly as a pint pot snubbing firkin.

"Can't go where?" we asked, not feeling any too kindly. Breakfast had been a complete flop because the compradore refused to supply kippers without cash.

"You can't go on the Bund without a pass."

"But I'm on the "North-China Daily News!"

"Can't help that. You can't go there without a pass."

We just showed him how it was done.

If newspapermen have to have passes for every place they go, they'll soon require a private secretary to carry the portfolio containing them.

* * *

Naivete

The man, Tang Wen-fu, was charged with espionage into the Chinese military positions in Chapei in disguise of a war refugee. A search on his person found two Japanese coins which are symbols given to Chinese "traitors" by the Japanese.—

In thus providing their spies with a ready means of identification by their captors the Japanese may be said to be giving just another example of true oriental courtesy.

* * *

A Brain Wave

We have been worried all night. First everything's been much too quiet for a man to get a wink of sleep, the pet poodle fidgets, and the chatter of the goldfish is enough to drive one crazy. Besides that we have been thinking. Thinking doesn't really come so difficult. All one has to do is just lie back, compose oneself, relax and . . . . well, just think. And it was the result of this thinking that led us to the discovery that we have a bone to pick with the Council.

The Council can't be expected to think of everything,—if they did poor In Parenthesis would have been out of a job long ago,—but as strategists they resemble the parboiled onion and as general peacemakers they have completely missed whatever bus has been running.

What In Parenthesis asks with all the gravity called forth by this unprecedentedly solemn occasion, what, he asks, has been done with the Municipal Orchestra? Why haven't its services been used in this present schemozzle? Here the Shanghai Municipal Council has had the most potent weapon at its disposal, and has failed to use it. Perhaps they have refrained from a desire not to take advantage of the weak, maybe in their strength they have felt that after all *noblesse oblige*, and, if it comes to that "*honi soit*," etc., applies in this instance. Or, perhaps, we have done them an injustice and they are reserving the Orchestra for bigger things.

Just think how a few days ago the Orchestra might have averted the cri . . . . schemozzle. The mind of a Machiavelli would have grasped the point at once. Fancy the effect of "Home, Sweet Home," upon the buzzums of the opposing forces, or "I'll sing the songs of Araby." Picture strong men on listening to one of Brahms' lullabies, throwing down their arms and weeping on each other's shoulders; fancy opponent commanders-in-chief sobbing over their maps, tearing them up and making telephone dates with the enemy for a petting party. In Parenthesis is quite certain, quite certain, mark you, that, if in this manner an appeal had been made to the better feelings of the men on both sides, the schemozzle would long ago have been transformed into a schemizzle.

But if it hadn't, what then? Well, is the repertoire of the Orchestra so limited? Could it not assume a sterner note? Of course it could. All the chairman of the Council would have had to do would have been to call up the officer commanding the Orchestra and simply say "Get busy; turn the fluence on." We could have had the Orchestra on the Race Course, sufficiently far away from human habitation, with loud speakers all along the perimeter of the Settlement, and at zero hour, after the contending forces had been given due warning to move on, hostilities could have been opened with a blast of Stravinsky—you know, a good old Straf,—followed by a heavy barrage of

THE NAKED SOVEREIGN

Respighi. Would the enemy fall back? You bet your sweet life they would, after which the orchestra could complete the rout with "Over the Hills and Far Away," or "My Bonny lies over the Ocean." If there are any objections on the score of brutality, it should be pointed out that the time has come to do away with false sentiment, and to indulge in a little ruthlessness. In Parenthesis has not copyrighted this idea and makes no charge for its use.

* * *

Answers to Correspondents

Etymologist.—A cactoblastis is not an engine of war. All that's happened to you is that you are getting mixed up in your swearing.

Sweet Alice.—Yes, he didn't arf do a Ben Bolt.

Foolish Too.—You ask "What are the wild waves saying?" Quite a lot since the permanent waves have gone away.

Anxious.—The next time he gets like that gently massage his head with a club.

Volunteer.—A good recipe for removing lip-stick? Cut it out kid: don't you realize there's a war on?

* * *

Oh! Wirra! Wirra! Wirra!

Scene, the Office, Enter a lad from the Ould Counthry one Cassidy by name.

"Could Oi be havin' a wurrud wid ye, sor."

"Why, of course, what can I do for you?"

"Oi wis thinkin' this marnin' if mebbe ye couldn't get me into this foight."

"However do you mean?"

"Couldn't ye be givin' me a bit letther to the Japanese commander inthroducin' me as a new recruit?"

"They wouldn't have you."

"And fer why, I'd be askin' ye."

"Because you are not Japanese."

"But phwat's the difference? Haven't the Oirish been foightn' for the English,—bad cess to 'em me mother always said,—fer hundreds uv years?"

"Yes, but there's no chance; they wouldn't have you."

"Do you think I could be jinin' the Chinese?"

"Whatever do you want to get mixed up in this mess for?"

"Mess is ut? Mess? Whoy it's the most iligint foight Oi've been seein' fer a long toime past. Couldn't ye just blarney the Chinese to lettin' me in? Oi wouldn't give much thrubble.

"But why?"

"Oi wis thinkin' Oi'd jist loike to jine in wid me little blackthorn here, to thry it out so to spake."

"You must understand, Cassidy. This is not a free-for-all: it's a private gentlemen's fight."

Och, a proivate gintlemen's foight! Whoi weren't ye after tellin' me that the first toime. No Oirish gintleman iver interfere's in a proivate gintlemen's foight. I'll be biddin' ye the top o' the marnin'. It's a bad wurruld. There's no taste o' peat in the potheen 'nd the Volunteers will not be afther lettin' me carry me blackthorn.

* * *

Proof Positive

From a local interview:—

Q. Won't the Japanese assume any responsibility for foreign property damaged?

A. The question is under consideration. Japan is not the only party in the dispute.

Q. I wish to press the point. What will Japan do if neutral nations carry arms to China. This is officially speaking not a war.

A. No, but it's a state of war.

Q. What do you consider a state of war.

A. When men shoot at each other.

Q. But no war has been declared.

A. But hostilities exist.

This is clear proof of what Ip has suspected for some considerable time that two certain countries don't love each other.

* * *

Moderation

A local contemporary writes:—

"Wednesday was a day of many rumours following the successful landing of Japanese troops at various points on the coast at the junction of the Yangtze and the Whangpoo Rivers, and many of the "news messages" sent out from various sources were not to be regarded as wholly reliable."

Our contemporary is quite gentle in dealing with the flagrant inexactitudes which have been published, but should remember that one of the first arts of war is to deceive the enemy. A really intensive programme such as is now embarked upon will leave the Japanese guessing as to whether they have retreated to Nagasaki or not.

"SAPAJOU" & "IN PARENTHESIS" OBSERVE THE WAR

SARDINE ROOM ONLY

Revelation

Just one of those profound thoughts which we never happen to think of ourself :—

"War is no respecter of individuals." You know we like that. It has about it a certain profundity, and all the indications of very deep thinking. Ip would like to hand a bouquet to the local writer who conceived so fine and true a statement. Yeah!

* * *

The Master Touch

Information from reliable sources reveal that as a result of the new situation at Woosung and outside Lotien, there has been some tactical redistribution of Chinese forces throughout the entire front.—" Central News."

There's a lot of information to be obtained from the above if one is good at perceiving the significance of the white spaces between the lines.

* * *

The Four Ds.

The Duchess is a lady,
  A dame of high renown,
But Danæ is a darling,
  The talk of all the town.
The way she flirts with Duncan
  Is everyone's Delight,
And we're wondering what will happen
  When they go out at night.

The Duchess, who's a lady,
  Says Danæ's surely not,
And speaks of her as being
  A thoroughly bad lot.
She rakes up that old story
  Of Danæ and god Zeus,
Who, as a golden shower, one day
  Got in and played the deuce.

Poor Duncan won't believe it;
  He says he'd rather not
Listen to his sweetheart called
  A nasty Greek harlot.
The Duchess says she doesn't care:
  She's launching an intrigue
To have the matter taken up
  By the Moral Welfare League.

Delight? She merely chuckles
  To hear the Duchess rant,
For, she says, " With warfare on
  Do that there 'ere you can't.
And still the Duchess raves on
  The situation's quirkish
Delight says " Keep your stays on, dear,
  For, as Delight, I'm Turkish!"

Good News
EGGS RESCUED IN HONGKEW

Behind that workmanlike heading lies a story which it falls to Ip. to tell. News having reached the authorities that $5,000,000 worth of food was in dire peril arrangements were made for its rescue, and the gentlemen who do everything from milking cows to herding swine were sent out, with the connivance of the Japanese to bring in the food supplies before they lost patience and walked in by themselves. The whole manœuvre was a complete success.

On reaching the storage place a strange sight met the rescuers. The butter was taking things quietly and the eggs on the whole were bearing up as well as could be expected. The sight of immediate relief, however, completely unmanned them. Hurrying from their boxes, thousands of eggs, brown eggs, white eggs, large eggs, small eggs, good eggs and bad eggs threw themselves on their knees and with hands clasped in supplication begged for immediate release. "Save us," they cried in unison, "Lest we all become addled." Henfruit, which in normal times maintains a sort of self-contained complacency, threw all reserve to the wind, and one particularly bad egg folding its arms round the Sergeant-major's neck, murmured coyly "Kiss me, my saviour!"

"Dear, dear, whispered the sergeant-major, as, overcome, he lapsed into regimental vernacular, and quickly seizing his pistol lanyard, strangled the poor wretch then and there.

Thousands upon thousands of eggs then filed out of the godown in orderly manner, hardly deigning to glance at the corpse of the comrade who had thus forgotten the convenances, while the sergeant-major, remarking that after all war *was* war, walked out behind them with a regimental " Hrrumph!"

* * *

This Very Strange World

From a local contemporary discussing Shanghai now so many of the women have evacuated :—

"And also he has the whole of the bathroom to himself where his own particular joy of splashing and singing is not marred by foolish remonstrance or gratuitous libel."

But,—er .... didn't he have the .... er .... bathroom .... er ... to himself before?

"SAPAJOU" & "IN PARENTHESIS" OBSERVE THE WAR

THIS ERA OF EXODUSES

"SAPAJOU" & "IN PARENTHESIS" OBSERVE THE WAR

The Oracle

"Asked whether or not he thought hostilities were over in the immediate Shanghai area, Mr. Fessenden declared that one man's guess is about as good as another's."

The above, suitably illuminated, with fine gold and red capitals, is being preserved as another of those revealing statements concerning the local situation.

* * *

A Word of Advice

Says Prince Konoye :—

"Japan's one course is to beat China to her knees so that she may no longer have the spirit to fight."

Care should be taken to see that there are still enough Chinese left alive to do the kneeling, —especially civilians.

* * *

Real Suffering

"Japan, Rear-Admiral Shimomura declared, wishes only to subdue the anti-Japanese elements, and had no desire of carrying on a war with China."

China may rest assured that it is more in sorrow than in anger that Japan has been obliged to adopt the course she has. Lachrymatory exhibitions on the part of the *cocodrillus vulgris* is mentioned by Maundev :—"Thes serpentes slen men and thei eten hem wepynge."

* * *

"There's Twenty-Thousand Cornishmen," etc.

"The spokesman of the Foreign Office, in Nanking, emphatically denies the report that Chinese troops will forcibly occupy the International Settlement in the course of their operations against the Japanese."

IN PARENTHESIS has discovered during a pleasant afternoon trip round the perimeter some thousands of reasons why this statement may be unreservedly accepted.

* * *

When This Unpleasant War Is Over

Old Timer in the correspondence columns yesterday writing about the dud bomb which fell at No. 30 Szechuen Road says :—

"The fragments recovered I understand comprise about 90 per cent of the total and I beg to suggest that the bomb be reconstructed and preserved by the S.M.C. in some museum or other as an historical piece."

Reading this a lump rose in IN PARENTHESIS's throat, as he pictured the reconstructed dud reposing in a museum surrounded by photographs of all the people it did not harm. We could start off with all the Council employees, posed after that famous if sickly picture "The Soul's Awakening" flanked by serried rows of ratepayers with expressions like those of the early Christian martyrs. That, of course, will come naturally when they find out how much this little spree is going to cost them. But Old Timer, if you think a dud bomb has any historical value, you should cut it out, kid : or take more water with it.

* * *

That Pain Again

This is the sort of thing which gives us all the symptoms of a contused neck :—

"While the tug-of-war between Chinese and Japanese forces continued yesterday in the Lotien area, etc. . . . ."

Now what we would like to know is how it is possible to have a tug-of-war with both sides advancing towards each other ?

* * *

Both Sides Still Winning

In a very short while, if sub-editors are obliged to walk as circumspectly as some people would have them, headings will become longer and longer, because of the safeguarding clauses which are becoming necessary in the presentation of the approximate truth. Thus, from a local contemporary :—

CONFLICTING REPORTS ON LOTIEN FRONT, WHERE

JAPANESE DECLARE THEY HAVE ADVANCED, WHILE CHINESE CLAIM PUSHBACK

Latest scoring :—

	Points	Errors Per cent	Hits
Ananias	42	100	nil
Sapphira	42	100	nil

* * *

Ambidextrous

London, Aug. 27.

After telephone consultations with the Foreign Secretary, Mr. Anthony Chamberlain, who is in Scotland, the Foreign Secretary, Mr. Anthony Eden, to-day decided what steps should

"SAPAJOU" & "IN PARENTHESIS" OBSERVE THE WAR

IS SHE ALSO EVACUATING?

"SAPAJOU" & "IN PARENTHESIS" OBSERVE THE WAR

be taken in regard to the shooting of the British Ambassador, Sir Hughe Knatchbull-Hugessen.

One of the most touching sights of the century must have been the Foreign Secretary talking to himself by telephone.

* * *

Naval Manœuvres

> "No sooner had the Chinese battery opened fire than the Idzumo swung into action."—War report.

Swinging into action, when moored fore and aft, is one of the most difficult feats known in navigation. It can only be done when the vessel is fitted with a double-jointed what's-its-names to the port and starboard rubbing strakes.

* * *

Our Dear Old S.M.C.

> "It would be entirely wrong to convey the impression that the emergency is over."—Broadcast.

It is blinding glimpses into the obvious like this that makes us love the Council more and more.

* * *

The Sub-Editor Again

COUPLE MARRY DESPITE
HOSTILITIES

Business as usual?

* * *

How About This One?

CHINESE PLANE REPORTED
GOING UP IN FLAMES

This trick has only been done once before, when a certain well known gentleman used a chariot.

* * *

The Scarlet Runner

In Parenthesis has interviewed the P.W.D. coolie working on The Bund, written about in Thursday's "N.C.D.N."

"Well, how's thing, old man?" we asked.

"Not so hot, Ip. not so hot."

"In what way."

"Well, if those sardine tins in the river would only keep quiet there may be a little bit of business to be picked up here and there." (Business with brush and kerosene tin pan) "I remember the time, mark you it was before all these stinking motor-cars came in, when men like me were kept busy from morning to night, picking up, picking up. But now? Why I haven't seen a horse since the week before last."

"I'm sure I don't know what can be done about it."

"I do."

"What?"

The old fellow looked at us with tears in his eyes: Couldn't you persuade the Commandant S.V.C., just once, to let the Light Horse ride down here, for a little while?"

* * *

News from the Front

A friendlier tone is creeping into the hostilities. Both sides having command of the air, it has been decided to share and share alike. One side will have command of the air during the day, and the other during the night. It is expected that this arrangement will receive the approbation of the League of Nations.

The end, it is reported is definitely in sight. Each side confidently expects to liquidate the situation in the course of the next few days.

* * *

A Small Wager

From a local contemporary, devoted to shopping matters:—

> "Major importers of foodstuffs insist that Shanghai has stocks on hand sufficient to last at least six months. Military traitors if caught, are taken out and shot, but far more despicable than the average military spy are the food profiteers who have already dug their vulturous beaks into the pocket books of local residents both foreign and Chinese. We believe that this sort of despicable thievery warrants the immediate attention of the proper authorities.

Ip cordially agrees with the above but he is willing to lay a bottle of grape fruit juice to a Crown cork stopper that nothing is done about it. Resort to the services of Capt. Boycott might prove useful. Vultures, of course, are quite respectable birds. They only take advantage of the dead—the compradores, the dead from the neck up.

* * *

These headings again

ENVOY WARNS
POWERS OF
TOKYO AIMS

That is one of the uses of envoys to reveal the obvious.

"SAPAJOU" & "IN PARENTHESIS" OBSERVE THE WAR

WILL THEY COLLIDE?

"SAPAJOU" & "IN PARENTHESIS" OBSERVE THE WAR

Sporting Notes

The fight between Tommy Farr and Joe Louis has been postponed because of threatening weather.

A gentle rain might also be expected to have a pacifying effect locally for few people can fire a rifle and hold up an umbrella at the same time.

* * *

Hospitality!

From the journal which advertizes "Come to Hongkong":—

> Experience has proved time and again that by pampering refugees their morale seriously deteriorates....
>
> But when it is remembered that the cost per head in an officers' mess in this Colony is half that which is being charged to the refugees, this fact naturally raises the query "Is the catering too lavish and/or too costly?"

" *Now all you poor blighters, just listen to me,*
When you've finished your bread and margarine tea,
Don't think that we grudge the food that you eat,
Or the brew that you've guzzled while we're standing treat:
Think not for a moment that some of you are
To be treated to things like black caviare.

" *You're just poor refugees; the sooner you know it*
Less food will you scoff, or in other words
'blow it.'
Excuse us if we, being perfectly frank,
Ask you 'Please don't toss round on that very soft plank,
Or wear out the windows by much looking through'
Poor, dear refugees, we're referring to you.

" *We don't try to be hard; for all that we do,—*
The unkinder we are,—the better for you,
It's your morale we think of. Just hand back that ham,
And stop those small children from wolfing the jam.
Do we think you're expensive? The answer is yes.
You cost twice as much as the officers' mess."

* * *

The Post Office

Readers will be pleased to know that the reason why they have received so little mail during the last two weeks is in no way due to any breakdown in the postal system, but simply because the letters have not been delivered.

In Hongkong

From a refugee's letter:—

> "Hongkong has lived up to its reputation for being sticky, for there was not one lady from any organization down to meet the boat to see it they could lend a hand."

CONVERSATION PIECE:—

I suppose, darling, you are going down to see the steamers come in?

Me? Whatever for?

To see all those refugees who have been evacuated from Shanghai.

Indeed no. I always think refugees are such a nasty class of people, if you understand what I mean.

Quate! But some of them might need assistance

Oh, well! What have we a port doctor for? Take my advice, dearest, don't have anything to do with them. You might catch something, — or something.

But I believe some of them are quate naice people.

Impossible dear. Refugees can nevah be naice people. What was it you called: three spades . . . ?

* * *

This War Complex

Really, local sub-editors should be more careful. War is war, it is readily admitted, but why introduce it into more peaceful matters? Thus a heading yesterday:—

> RADIO BROADCAST OF S.M.C. STRIKES OPTIMISTIC NOTE

We don't suppose it did anything of the sort. It probably *sounded* the note in question.

* * *

Rhetoric!

> Only in this way can we refill the ranks of national leaders who are to-day risking their personal lives for the salvation of China.

Something will also have to be done to fill the ranks of the national leaders who are risking their impersonal lives.

* * *

A Dementi

How we like that world *démenti*—sounds so frightfully diplomatic, don't you think or do you? However, joking apart, IN PARENTHESIS is in a position to state that there is no political or military significance in the concentration of Chinese personages at Bad Nauheim.

"SAPAJOU" & "IN PARENTHESIS" OBSERVE THE WAR

DECLARED OR UNDECLARED—WHAT IS THE DIFFERENCE?

"SAPAJOU" & "IN PARENTHESIS" OBSERVE THE WAR

An Inquiry

We should dearly like to know the name of the man who staggered into the bar and called for a bin-and-jitters!

* * *

The Tin Hat

Last Friday, dealing with the office tin hat we went on record to the effect that that was the day we had our turn to duck under it. Since then we have been supplied with one of our very own. Sunday being out day off—strict trade union, we are, forty-hour week, you know, and one day off,—we bathed the canary in it in the morning, and gave a sukiyaki party that night. If we can only get hold of another we shall be equipped with a sitz bath.

* * *

War Reporting

The censor is quite busy in Japan, chiefly for the purpose of preventing people knowing that there is a war on in China. At least that is how it started. Now, of course, greater care has to be taken in newspaper accounts published there to prevent the Chinese ascertaining the whereabouts of certain Japanese units. Thus an account taken from the " Japan Chronicle : "—

> Mr. Paul Amos, a Princeton student, supplies the following extracts from his diary of events of last week-end :—
>
> " Most of us pack before lunch in anticipation of evacuating at short notice. We decided to move as soon after lunch as possible. After two or three of us finished packing we started off to the Palace Hotel ; we had been there half an hour when four of us started to play bridge, but I thought I would go to the Bund to get a better view of the excitement ... I saw five Chinese aeroplanes flying towards the—which was firing its anti-aircraft batteries while the Chinese on the wharf were clapping and cheering the arrival of their planes.
>
> " Looking up I saw more planes directly overhead. The—again fired.

IN PARENTHESIS, desiring to be perfectly fair to both sides, naturally refrains from publishing the fact that it was the " Idzumo " the Chinese aviators were trying to bomb. Up to the present it is believed that the Chinese do not know where the vessel is.

The Terrors of War

Most of you people in Shanghai do not realize the terrible times you are going through. The following from the " Japan Times," of August 20, ought to let you know what you are suffering.

> Shanghai is suffering from a serious shortage of food, and the water is said to be running low. Thousands of Chinese refugees have been driven frantic, and are mobbing stores and other places where food can be obtained.

Trying to make our flesh creep like this is definitely unfair.

* * *

This English

> Nanking, Aug. 30.—Chinese circles are most indignant at the Japanese allegation that Chinese aeroplanes camouflaged as Japanese are carrying out bombing operations.
>
> A Chinese army spokesman branded the allegation as a " pure, deliberate fabrication."—Reuter.

Deliberate we agree, but " pure "? A fabrication can never be pure. Of course what the spokesman wanted to say was that it was a dirty lie, which is perfectly good English.

* * *

The Advice Giver

The following is from an article by Mr. F. C. Millington in the " China Mail."

> I had already suggested to the Council that they should broadcast the truth each day and I was pleased to see that they had decided to do this just as I left, seven days late, but better late than never as this will definitely stop the rumours going out over the air. Why did they wait till all the women had left before they follow my advice? They did not follow my advice re a Council Chinese newspaper but this doesn't matter so very much if they go on the air with authentic news, though I still maintain that an official Chinese news bulletin would do nothing but good and would make the papers take great care with what they decided to publish.

Mr. Millington arrived in Hongkong in the s.s. Maron.

"SAPAJOU" & "IN PARENTHESIS" OBSERVE THE WAR

SIMPLE, MY DEAR WATSON!

"SAPAJOU" & "IN PARENTHESIS" OBSERVE THE WAR

How Truly Oriental!

From an editorial in a local contemporary:—

> "It is reported that the Japanese in Tsingtao are contemplating the placing of their properties and industrial plants in the custody of the Chinese municipal authorities. The idea is the same as that carried out in Hankow ... The Chinese may be gentlemen in war as in peace, but the Japanese cannot expect to make simpletons of them at all times."

Japan to China.—Here, just hold my coat for a moment, while I paste you on the jaw!

* * *

Municipal Health

From a local contemporary:—

> Health authorities in both the Settlement and Concession are being inspected and sanitated daily.

The sight of one of our health officials being daily sanitated is one of the things we have yet to see.

* * *

On Cooking

Something we do not like to see in a cookery book:—Take three-quarters of a cupful of freshly shelled peas.... It always makes us wonder what they have done to be treated that way.

* * *

The War Situation

IN PARENTHESIS and his experts have been able to make a complete study of the present state of the war and have come to the following conclusions:—

Both sides have still command of the air, one side, of course more than the other and the other less than the other, if you get what we mean.

As a result of widespread movements during the past week each side may be said to have outflanked the other. This is a most difficult feat in warfare, but when achieved means that the opponents have to stop and start all over again. Otherwise they would be occupying each other's positions, which, naturally, is never done.

Another phenomenal feat which is constantly being performed is that each side is holding the enemy. No one, for a moment, would suggest that they can't leave go, but most military, and for that matter naval, observers, are agreed that such is the case.

Both sides are reported to be satisfactorily liquidating the situation—hic!

As things are at present the front line may be said to be more or less static, with both sides facing different ways; directly they face the same way one of them will be in retreat. On this point we are in complete agreement with Clausewitz, Norman Angell and George Bernard Shaw.

Interviewed by the Press the spokesman of a certain army said "We shall strike while the iron's hot." Writers of most military textbooks are emphatic that it is no good striking while the iron's cold.

It is also confidently expected that both sides will repulse the enemy. These are what are called repulsive tactics.

* * *

Safer Shanghai

What with earthquakes, typhoons, epidemics, etc., which we read of in other places, Shanghai doesn't seem so bad, even though there are about a quarter of a million men round the place not on speaking terms.

* * *

Political Note

The Seiyukai party are demanding that the Japanese government should adopt a more positive policy towards China.—There has not been anything very negative about it up to the present.

* * *

La donna e mobile

PERSONAL

GENTLEMAN I met Wednesday morning before troubles and left corner Museum and Hongkong Road is requested communicate with all details.

> She left him right in Hongkong Road,
>   And flounced upon her heel:
> Remarked he was a nasty toad,
>   So sick he made her feel
> She left him flat.
>
> But beauty in a gentler mood,
>   To loving kindness given,
> Dislikes a breaking heart to brood,
>   And seeks to mend the riven
> So that is that!

* * *

What's in a Name?

> Tokyo, Sept. 2.—The Cabinet to-day decided to change the terminological description of the current crisis from

DANCE MACABRE

"SAPAJOU" & "IN PARENTHESIS" OBSERVE THE WAR

"North China Incident" to "China Incident."—Domei.

This momentous decision having been reached it will now be possible to get on with things.

* * *

Diplomatic Note

IN PARENTHESIS understands that a Note registering the strongest possible protest against the weather which Siccawei has been supplying during the past week or so is being prepared. It may not be possible to beat Siccawei to its knees, but it may be necessary to remind it that with a war on it is necessary that the fighters should be kept as cool as possible. Besides the convenience of subscribers to ringside seats has also to be borne in mind.

* * *

Uneasy Hongkong

The "South China Morning Post's" humourist:—

> Nothing amusing about it, of course, but one wonders what effect the Shanghai migration will have upon Hongkong's economics, opinions, morals, and smugness. Future generations of taipans may have a lot of work to blame this war for.

We of course are not worrying about the morals of our evacuees, but we do hope they will be able to keep themselves clean.

* * *

Disillusionment

A local editor writes:—

> Within the perimeter, Shanghai has done wonderfully during the past few days in trying to get back to a calmer and more ordered state, especially as the noise of battle has been out of range. *But it is neither pessimistic nor alarmist to point out that we are still very much within a war zone . . . .*

Oh! Go hon! We thought we had moved!

* * *

A Disclaimer

Contrary to evilly inspired rumours IN PARENTHESIS wishes emphatically to state that he is not in the pay of either side to this present conflict. Worse luck.

* * *

Another Complaint

The heartless disregard by the Japanese naval units of the ordinary convenience of neutral foreigners was again evidenced yesterday. The boy was just pouring one out when one of the shells exploded on Pootung Point. We didn't mind our pants being wetted, but we did object to the wanton waste of good whisky.

* * *

A Story with a Moral

A dog carrying a bone in his mouth was walking over a bridge across a stream, when looking down he saw his reflection in the water. Thinking it was another dog, and admiring the size of his bone, he said "Gimme" and dropped his own bone in the water.

The moral of this little story is that you should never speak with your mouth full.

* * *

Recruiting Swells

Is a heading given by a contemporary to an item of news regarding the British Army. Swells fire rifles just as well as the common peepul.

* * *

Correspondence

IN PARENTHESIS
  "NORTH-CHINA DAILY NEWS"

Dear I.P.:—

When is a war not a war?
When it's an incident.

When is China really sincere?
When she admits she's wrong (though right).

What resembles closely "Pear's baby reaching for the soap"?
Japan. Because she won't be happy till she gets it (China).

When will China learn to understand Japan's good intentions?
When she kneels down, after she's lost all her soil.

S. Y. S.

Shanghai, Sept. 3.

* * *

The Wonder-workers

A local contemporary who early in hostilities discovered that

"War is no respecter of persons,"

went on record yesterday as also having found out that

"War is no respecter of individuals."

Two such discoveries in three weeks is pretty good going, and there need be no fear for journalism if similar revelations continue to be made at this rate.

"SAPAJOU" & "IN PARENTHESIS" OBSERVE THE WAR

DOUBLE SUICIDE?

BRASS AND STRINGS

"SAPAJOU" & "IN PARENTHESIS" OBSERVE THE WAR

The Blow Falls
On Saturday night at dinner a fellow had to pull the remark about Nero, of which we so strongly disapprove. The body has been embalmed, funeral arrangements to be announced later.

* * *

A Sad Thought
It's astonishing how evil companionship corrupts things. Just fancy only yesterday we were reading about shot and shell falling, and now we have it on perfectly good authority that night fell yesterday.

* * *

The Stylist
"The craft burst into flames and plunged like a spear to terra firma . . . ."

There is not the slightest doubt about the fact that this war is bringing all that is best out of our local descriptive writers.

* * *

Whose Fault Now?
The undertaking that the bombing planes of a certain nation would not fly over the foreign areas is being scrupulously observed. If, however, those areas should be foolish enough as to get under the planes in question no responsibility for what may happen can be accepted.

* * *

Tenderer
This war is affecting some people in peculiar ways. One man is now so averse from cruelty that he insists that his boy shall anæsthetize his eggs before putting them in boiling water.

* * *

And Talking of Eggs
We don't know whether it was amongst those recently rescued or not, but one we had the other morning had ceased to take any interest whatever in the war. Its mind was set on higher things.

* * *

Technical Note
Some of the artillery practice we have seen during the past week was in its way unique. Shells fell as far from their targets as the length of the range over which they were fired. This, of course, may be due to a hundred-and-one reasons, any one of which may be perfectly good. The first, however, is the best.

Auntie Says
Well, boys and girls, we are now entering upon the fourth week of the war. It hardly seems to be three weeks since certain people started playing the giddy goat round the perimeter but there it is.

We were talking over the situation yesterday, being Sunday, with our stenographer, Miss Ipplethwick, whom you already know.

"My," she said, licking the point of her pencil, as all good stenographers do. "My, but I don't know what will happen when peace comes again. I haven't had a date since the war broke out. My boy's in the Volunteers, saving his money, or at least I hope so, and I don't know one end of a rhumba from other."

"Yes, but what do you think of the political situation?" we asked.

"Well," she replied, "I don't sort of rightly know, if you get what I mean. But I've been talking it over with auntie and she says it's no good trying to give a man a swift kick in the pants, if he can manage to give you a severe wallop in the wallet, so to speak."

* * *

Military Note
Judging from the results obtained some of the artillerymen operating round Shanghai would make good market gardeners.

* * *

Customs' Little Joke
CUSTOMS NOTIFICATION

No. 1605

The public is hereby notified that, in accordance with Government instructions, the export abroad and to Manchuria and Dairen of the following articles is temporarily prohibited.

Beans and Peas of all kinds,
Buckwheat,
Kaoliang (Sorghum),
Maize, ffi
Millet, and
Cereals, n.o.p.f.

Now anyone who can export beans and peas of all kinds, buckwheat, kaoliang (sorghum), maize, ffi., millet and cereals, n.o.p.f. from Shanghai to Manchuria and Dairen just now, could produce rabbits from a hat without even having a hat.

* * *

A Protest
We do wish people would refrain from writing in complaining about the postal service.

"SAPAJOU" & "IN PARENTHESIS" OBSERVE THE WAR

A FRIEND IN NEED?

—AND THERE IS NO FIRE-ENGINE!

The fact that everyone is not getting all the mail he would like means nothing at all to our fair young life. All we've had have been love letters stating that unless we paid up in three days . . . Well you know the story. It may rightly be said of the Chinese Post Office that, with true oriental courtesy, it is tempering the wind to the shorn sheep.

* * *

Interlude

This war's becoming a riot. Amongst other refugees which have been admitted to the office since the outbreak, the latest to arrive has been someone's radio set. Unfortunately it works. We caught one of the sub-editors doing some fancy dancing with Miss Ipplethwick on Saturday, while a shroff who dropped in was entertained to "Kiss me again."

* * *

These Amateur Strategists

From a local war correspondent:—

> The fact remains that if the Japanese actually succeed in landing 100,000 men in the Shanghai area *it is hardly likely that they will withdraw before they have been thoroughly defeated or attained substantial gains.* The frequent information regarding such large reinforcements lends weight to the theory that the Japanese are pondering an extensive inland campaign, possibly with Nanking as the objective.

There is, of course, just a possibility that they will not withdraw in either event. In the case of the first they might remain to avenge their reverse, while as for the second what is the use of making substantial gains and then giving them up?

* * *

Cause for Rejoicing

One good thing this war has brought us. No one has told us anything this year about the Hangchow bore.

* * *

Behind the Scenes

In Parenthesis doesn't mind admitting that he was responsible for the quiet which prevailed on Sunday. It was with the greatest reluctance that he had to summon the high commands to a conference over the show they are putting up. There was a certain amount of stiffness about the proceedings at the commencement, but Ip. decided that the only thing was to tell them where they got off.

"Looka here, you fellers," he remarked transferring his well-chewed cigar from starboard to port. "You've got this show all wrong. Don't you understan' your public wants action. Why, that lousy little one-horse show in Spain has been playing to full houses for the past year, and you fellers with all the talent in the world aren't doing any better than a one night stand.

"Yer fires was pretty good, and that entr'act on Friday was the snake's hips, but believe me, or believe me not, when you ain't got a beauty chorus—and that's a pity because I reckon a leg show has the box office beat—you've gotta givem sumpin'. fer their money."

"Well, what do you suggest?"

Fr'instance, why not open each day's programme with an overture? Izzy could put in plenty of oompah, oompah on the Whangpoo, and all the rest could come it with their instruments. Believe me, boys, if we can't give 'em legs, we gotta give 'em noise.

"If you are referring to the Izumo, allow me to inform you that the vessel's name is not Izzy."

"Oh, yeah? Well Izzy looks better on the bill anyhow, and I tell yer again you've got to think of yer public. Make the show snappy, keep the audience thinking how good it is, and even if its rotten they'll like it. And how? And think of the noospapers. Do you think all these fellers here want to telegraph their home papers just to say the day was quiet. Why boys, unless you speed things up a bit, you'll be off the front page, and only wriggle in as a three line par. Be yourselves, lads. Remember what my old father used to tell me. In jobs like this nothing succeeds like excess. But, you know, I still think it's a pity you haven't got a leg show. Makes things brighter to my mind."

As you will doubtless remember things moved a bit faster yesterday morning, but Ip has warned them that unless they get more snap into their turns, he'll definitely take the show off.

* * *

There's Still Hope

> "The Japanese Naval authorities are giving consideration to the reopening of a 'major British-owned brewery in the Yangtszepoo District,' a Japanese naval spokesman announced yesterday.
>
> "'This special consideration,' he said, 'was being given in view of the gravity of the situation on the beer front.'"

When people start joking about beer, it merely serves to show how serious matters really

"SAPAJOU" & "IN PARENTHESIS" OBSERVE THE WAR

VIGNETTES OF SHANGHAI LIFE

"SAPAJOU" & "IN PARENTHESIS" OBSERVE THE WAR

are. Beer, like mothers-in-law should never be joked about; they are the two main pillars of our civilization. The next time the Japanese naval spokesman pulls a swift one about either of these subjects IN PARENTHESIS will report him to the League of Nations.

* * *

Nervous

Then there's the other man on the staff who refuses to come to work. Says he can't stand the rattle of the typewriters.

* * *

Literary Thought

Wasn't it Julius Caesar, or some other great thinker, who said he'd rather have a pair of roller skates in Hampstead than a cycle in Cathay?

* * *

Laconic

Wife safe elsewhere cabling to husband doing a job of work in Shanghai:—Am worried over your safety.

Husband's reply:—So am I.

* * *

The Situation to Date

There has been little to report on the various war fronts over the week-end. Roughly speaking the position seems to be this:—Unless there is a change things will remain very much as they are.

* * *

Determination

After studying the declarations of the various Japanese statesmen it is impossible to escape the conclusion that Tokyo is determined to make China a friendly nation. In other words China is going to be made to like Japan and . . . . er, like it!

* * *

The Realist

"What I have always said," remarked the pacifist, "is that if we could only get the two countries together all this trouble would be settled."

"Hell!" replied the cynic, "Seems to me they can't be any closer together than they are right now."

* * *

The Unconscious Humourist

Tokyo, Sept. 6. (Domei)

The current Sino-Japanese hostilities will come to an end when the two countries come to an agreement and there is no further need for armed action, Finance Minister Okinori Kaya said in the Diet to-day.

We do not remember having ever seen the matter put so plainly before.

* * *

Answers to Correspondents

Anxious.—Yes, we heard that big noise yesterday morning. It was the sound of one of the opposing parties "dropping a brick."

Statistician.—The number of Japanese transports outside the mouth of the Yangtze has not yet been ascertained. There are probably more than the Japanese will admit and less than some people think. If you take the average between the two you should be just about correct.

* * *

These War Correspondents

Devastation worse than anything produced by the World War is visible on every side in Hongkew and Chapei, a Reuter Special correspondent found when he went behind the Japanese lines yesterday during the battle of the Yangtzsepoo.

Shot and shell were flying about haphazardly and the boom and crash of trench mortar shells seemed just round the corner.

World war veterans will be interested to learn how much more terrible has been the devastation across the Soochow Creek than that which disfigured the towns of France. Judging, however, from some of the artillery work we have seen, it is just possible that shot and shell *were* flying about haphazardly.

* * *

She's Back Again

Little Audrey dropped in yesterday dressed in Chinese clothes, and not too good at that.

"Got a cigarette, Ip?" she asked.

"Certainly. But what's the idea? Why the Chinese habiliments?"

"I'm helping the Chinese in this show."

"Whatever do you mean. If you'd had a grain of sense you would have evacuated to Hongkong weeks ago."

"Yes, and have been vaccinated, inocculated and segregated. Believe me, big boy, when I want to be shot, no Hongkong squirt is going to do it with a hypodermic, when there are nice big guns about to do it properly."

"Well, what have you been doing?"

"SAPAJOU" & "IN PARENTHESIS" OBSERVE THE WAR

TOPICAL SOUNDS

"SAPAJOU" & "IN PARENTHESIS" OBSERVE THE WAR

"I'm a Chinese irregular. Didn't you see me last Friday. I was yulohing my sampan down the river, near the Idzumo. Say, did those lads get a scare?"

"What were you doing there?"

"Well, you see, I was a bit sore over my failure to torpedo Izzy a few weeks ago, and I was sort of looking things over again, when they opened fire on me."

"But weren't you afraid?"

"Yes, terribly. The way they were carrying on might have made me late for lunch."

"But I mean all that machine-gunning, and the bombardment—"

"The bombardment was not so good. I got pieces of shrapnel in my hair, which took the amah quite a time to get out afterwards. But the shooting didn't worry me."

"Why didn't it?"

"The only way they'll ever hit a target with a machine-gun is to fix bayonets and charge." And Little Audrey left the room smiling gently.

* * *

Reassuring

While Chinese Customs vessels will be seized, the spokesman said, lightships and other Government-owned ships "playing a major rôle in the maintenance of international trade routes" will not be interfered with by the Japanese Navy.

The point being, of course, that even Japanese war shipping likes to know where it is,—if and when. You understand, if and when they don't know.

* * *

The Sword of Damocles

It was a bit of a blow to some local residents to wake up on Tuesday to find that their wives, whom they thought safe in Hongkong, had just breezed in on the d'Artagnan. One man, who was caught having breakfast with a sizzling blond, is still explaining to the missis how it all came about.

* * *

The Truth at Last

As a result of the exchange of diplomatic correspondence between Whitehall and Tokyo on the subject of the shooting of the British Ambassador considerable light has been thrown on the matter. It is now perfectly clear that the Chinese, must have been gunning and bombing their own lines of communication. It is, of course, a discovery new to military science but is said to have a certain successful effect in completely surprising the enemy.

The New Projectile

Judging from some of the sand-bagging that is going on round town, foreign inhabitants seem to be highly impressed by the new shell which one of the combatants is using. This missile, invented by Professor Egbert George Whoosit, branches off at right-angles in its flight, thereby greatly deceiving the enemy.

* * *

These British Again

They do tell the story of the British officer who entered a local store to buy some prickly heat medicine, and had laid his cap aside to apply some to his forehead, when an American Marine came in. He was most interested in the cap, picked it up and was moving off with it when the officer remonstrated.

"Oh!" said the marine, "You're British! I thought you were some foreign troops."

* * *

By the name of Jones

It is reported, with what authority it is not clear, that in one of the platoons in the Welch Fusiliers of thirty-two men twenty-six answer to the name of Jones.

It doesn't seem that anything can be done about it.

* * *

Correspondence

IN PARENTHESIS
"NORTH-CHINA DAILY NEWS"

DEAR I.P. :—

It seems that Japanese dictionaries have different definitions from those of other countries. A school boy in Japan upon consulting his dictionary apparently sees the following:

Incident—an altercation with a neighbouring country which costs us £1,000,000 a day.

Sincerity—a trait which only we possess, and which therefore only we know the meaning of.

Co-operation—acts—performed by another country after bombs, shells, and bayonets have made our meaning clear.

Defensive (war)—(war) which is fought entirely outside our own territory.

War—(This word is omitted from the dictionary, because Japan having signed the Kellogg Pact "never under any circumstances to resort to the use of force" has no need for such a word).

Non-combatant—(This word is also omitted).

"SAPAJOU" & "IN PARENTHESIS" OBSERVE THE WAR

AN "INCIDENTAL" MATCH

Army, Navy—those who have taken upon themselves the sole responsibility for preserving peace, and who accept no help in the performance of their duty.

Premier—one who is entirely subservient to the Army and Navy.

Treaties—something which China must observe.

Philanthropist—(This is the only word whose meaning corresponds to that given in dictionaries of other countries, and one definition is—those who through humanitarian motives give aid to the neutral and enemy needy).

WOULD-BE LEXICOGRAPHER

Shanghai, Sept. 9.

* * *

Proof Positive

The Chinese air-raid of Wednesday evening conclusively proves that our experts have been correct all along in claiming that both sides have command of the air.

* * *

Scene at Headquarters

Commanding Officer.—Have we landed everything now?

Chief of Staff.—Yes, sir.

C.O.—Have the men been fed?

C.O.S.—They have.

C.O.—And has the Regimental Sergeant-Major made perfectly sure that all ranks have washed behind the ears this morning.

C.O.S.—All examined and found correct.

C.O.—And are all the Press photographers present?

C.O.S.—They are.

C.O.—And the special correspondents, too?

C.O.S.—Yes, sir. All of them.

C.O.—Very well. Give the order to advance.

* * *

Definition

It is frequently to be noticed in communiqués that claims are made that the enemy have been repelled. Amongst lecturers at the staff colleges this is known as repellant behaviour.

* * *

Social Note

It is expected that, shortly, social Shanghai will be rocked by the revelations to be made in a local divorce court. It all arises out of the wife's persistence in knitting during the war. The sound made when she drops a stitch has completely unnerved the husband who is suing on the ground of cruelty.

The Merry Thought

Dear I.P at this moment solemn
I offer this tale to your precious colunm.
Each day to the ' Front ' I've hied,
Sitting at the ' boy friend's ' side;
Likewise every day at four
You'd find me at his office door.
Imagine then my consternation;
When he received an invitation,
One afternoon at half-past-three
To a game of billiards and a cup o' tea.
I calmly said, without a fuss,
' That's all right I'll take the bus.'
We stopped outside the A.P.C.
And said good-bye most tenderly.
The Bund was quiet and rather eerie;
I felt Creepy! Queerly! Weary!
When all at once with glad surprise,
The name of the building caught my eyes;
No longer was I feeling dizzy
I felt as safe as little ' Izzy.'
' SHELL BUILDING ' were the words I read,
Ah! I was safe, and far from dead;
For the things which command to be ' Shelled and Shot '
Are the jolly old things which are D—d well not.

From "The Girl He Left Behind."

* * *

The Rumour Hound

He came up to us in the club the other evening, with the fixed look in his eye—you know the sort of thing: the look which the official spokesman assumes when he is going to put over a particularly fast one—and grabbing us by the lapel of our coat started :—

"Have you heard . . . ."

"Don't, please don't tell us," we pleaded. "Don't make our blood curdle any more."

"But you don't know what I am going to say."

"Oh, yes. I do."

"Well what is it then, if you're so smart?"

"I know. The big push is going to start to-morrow. You have got it on the best authority. Indeed right out of the horse's mouth."

"Well, it isn't exactly that. That big push I know definitely is to start to-morrow, but believe it or not, the Japanese boast that they will have at least one-hundred-and-sixty-two aeroplanes in the air."

"You don't say."

"Yes. One-hundred-and-sixty-two."

"Uh! I should worry. Seems to me they couldn't be in a better place than in the air."

"But fancy one-hundred-and-sixty-two!"

"Are you sure of your fact."

SHANGHAI-WOOSUNG CHAMPIONSHIP

"SAPAJOU" & "IN PARENTHESIS" OBSERVE THE WAR

"Absolutely, ol' man. I've got a friend whose amah's first cousin works in an egg factory, and she says it is bound to come to-morrow. You know I don't like that number."

"Neither do I."

"Why not?"

"Well for one thing you can't divide it by four, and if you could what's the use?"

Then gently disengaging his grip on our coat, and avoiding the fixity of his eye we knocked one back. Just to keep our spirits up.

* * *

Ingenious

Amongst other important items of news which In Parenthesis has been able to glean is an account of the new aeroplane which is shortly to be imported by China, for the purpose of dealing with the enemy.

This wonderful new machine has been so built that the aviator can fly backwards whenever he fears to get dust in his eyes. It also serves the double purpose of confounding the enemy who can never be quite sure whether the 'plane is coming or going.

* * *

Those Communique writers

Tokyo, Sept. 9.

Twenty-two machines were lost by the Japanese Navy in the course of aerial engagements and raids on important Chinese centres between August 13 and to-day, the Admiralty announced to-night.

This number, the communiqué added, included planes which failed to return from raids, but no definite information as to whose fate has been received.

The Chinese aerial losses were put by the Navy at 194 planes, shot down or destroyed at Chinese aerodromes.

The method of ascertaining the number of aeroplanes destroyed in Chinese aerodromes is unique. It is done by multiplying the time of the day with the day of the month, subtracting the aviator's age and adding the first number you think of. This method is more or less correct.

* * *

How Unfortunate

Report from a fire brigade expert sent to deal with a burning oil tank:—"I am in a pregnant position with thousands of tons of oil around me."

The Prevailing Mode

Paraguay determined to be in the fashion has declared a state of war to prevail. This seems somewhat drastic, for your really modish nations avoid going to such extremes, It is so much more companionable to shoot people down sociable-like.

* * *

S. O. S.

Dear I. P this awful ' War '
Has very nearly got me ' sore,'
Won't you be a ' Dorothy Dix'
And Wiggle me out of a terrible fix.
'twas ' Bloody Saturday ' very late,
With my chum I did evacuate.
We joined a very long procession,
To rent a flat in the French Concession.
All was quiet and simply 'spiffin,'
My boy friend asked us both to tiffin;
' She no b'long ploper Shanghai Girl,'
She makee all same clazy whirl.'
He takes her out instead of me,
And between us we possess one key.
Now don't you think this is a sin?
I must wait up nights and let her in.
Could the Council put the Curfew back?
My beauty sleep I sadly lack;
Would you suggest an appeal to ' Izzy '
To cure his character so ' fizzy '
What would you do? Oh! Please be kind,
And help.

THE GIRL HE LEFT BEHIND.

* * *

Completely Misunderstood

The practice which some nations have adopted of sending unconscious humourists abroad to represent them in consular capacities does not always have the happiest results. Thus the Japanese Consul-General in New York has been doing some fancy talking:—

> "But if anyone thinks the trouble was made by the Japanese alone for the object of conquest, he is entirely mistaken."

That's what we have always contended. If people would only follow intelligently what we have written they would realize that the present incident is for the sole purpose of endeavouring to persuade China to take Manchoukuo back.

* * *

The Situation

The experts engaged by IN PARENTHESIS have again been looking the situation over, and to be perfectly frank, they don't like it.

"SAPAJOU" & "IN PARENTHESIS" OBSERVE THE WAR

LOOKING AHEAD

"SAPAJOU" & "IN PARENTHESIS" OBSERVE THE WAR

One of the most perplexing developments during the past week has been the sudden invasion of wives from Hongkong, most of whom made a successful landing on Tuesday morning. This was chiefly due to surprise tactics for many of the local defenders had no knowledge of the impending descent.

Apart from that there is very little to report. Both sides have been continually advancing, and it is firmly believed that a large scale movement will have to be undertaken for the purpose of getting them back to where they started from.

A strong protest has been lodged with the board of referees, it being alleged against one of the opposing teams that he kicked off before the whistle blew. That, of course, is entirely contrary to the spirit of the game.

Statements made by spokesmen on both sides indicate that every effort is still being made to prevent the present situation developing into warfare. The peaceful sentiments expressed on both sides are said to be most encouraging.

No definite date has been fixed for the big push. Directly it is successful it will have started, but up to the present both commands have been busily engaged in endeavouring to discover a propitious day.

* * *

Outrageous

Tokyo, Sept. 10, (UP) "Domei News Agency" to-day published a dispatch from Lotien claiming that 500 girl Communists trained in Nanking by Mme. Sun Yat-sen were permeating the Chinese army, teaching Communist doctrines, encouraging the soldiers to fight the Japanese and observing strict military discipline.

We can quite understand Japanese indignation over the whole matter, for it is very unmaidenly of these damsels to encourage the soldiers to fight the Japanese, who are so anxious to prove to the Chinese how really friendly they feel.

* * *

The Brute

A correspondent writes:—"It must be frightfully difficult finding things to be funny about nowadays." You betcher! It's quite all right when Izzy wants to "poop" off at Pootung, or when everyone joins in to strafe a raiding aeroplane. But there's a man working on a building a few doors away who insists on dropping a plank on the roof every few minutes. The fellow's got no sense of humour. That's what he hasn't.

The War

Is proceeding exactly to schedule. On Fridays we regularly bombard Pootung. Last week was no exception. Indeed the programme of these hostilities is just like the boarding house menus. We always know what we're going to get to-morrow.

* * *

Revelation

Japan's fundamental national policy is co-operation with China. Prince Fumimaro Konoye said to-day in an official message addressed to the nation.— "News Message."

As far as we can see the Chinese have been rendering every possible co-operation in this present shindy, for every time Japanese shoot at them they shoot back. What more could anyone want?

* * *

Advice to The Girl he left Behind

My dear I.P. you must admit,
The girl friend's had a nasty hit.
She asks, should she appeal to ' Izzy ' !
But is 'e truly worth it, is 'e
Good enough in pre-war days?
For now's the chance to ' Part the ways.'
' Izzy ' cannot give advice;
She's tried to catch 'em once or twice;
A ' shot ' from such a source as that,
Would ' bomb ' the love affair quiet flat.
Besides with all the lads about,
The girl should have no cause to shout.
With not a mother-in-law in sight,
How has she got in such a plight?
' Give the Chum one little date.
(I hear she's to evacuate)
Take the advice of ' Dorothy Dix '
Give his cocktail a stronger ' mix.'
And if the ' Boy Friend's ' not quite blind
He'll return to The Girl He left Behind.

* * *

Our Marksmen

We thought of this on Saturday morning as we watched the air-raid:—The chief fault of the gentlemen manipulating the anti-aircraft artillery is that they shoot at where the aeroplanes come from instead of where they anticipate they are going. This, of course, is not wise, unless they are trying not to hurt each other.

"SAPAJOU" & "IN PARENTHESIS" OBSERVE THE WAR

AN EXPERT OPINION

"SAPAJOU" & "IN PARENTHESIS" OBSERVE THE WAR

The Spread of War
JAPANESE CLAIM ADVANCES ON ALL SHANGHAI FRONTS

Chinese Say Line Held At Every Point

CONFLICTING RUMOURS OF FIGHTING

Now that even rumours are in conflict with each other an extension of hostilities may be expected at any moment!

* * *

This Queer World

Readers should note that the incidents and characters mentioned below are entirely fictitious, and unbelievable as it may seem, have no reference whatever to known localities or personalities.

Scene.—Council Chamber of Worpington-cum-slushpuddle with Council in session.

Chairman.—And now, Mr. Clerk what's the next business?

Clerk.—An application from Mr. Yu Kum-on to evacu . . . . to secure possession of 200 cases of sardines at present in a go . . . . warehouse in Yang . . . . that district at present inaccessible and under the fire of two co-operating nations. Mr. Yu needs the sardines in his business.

Councillor Dogsbody.—And wot I arsks is sardines? Are they necessary for the sustenance of life?

Chairman.—Sardines are fish. You know, I always feel so sorry for them when a tin is opened—such cramped quarters, if you get what I mean. Mr. Yu is a grocer, and like all gentlemen in his line of business has been carrying on as usual.

Councillor Dogsbody.—Yus at 'igher prices. Grindin' the fyces of the poor at a time like this. Wot? I arsks. Wot are you again' ter do abart it?

Clerk.—It was suggested that we should detail the village constable to proceed to the area in question to escort a lorry protected by the local band and secure the sardines to be handed over to Mr. Yu.

Councillor Dogsbody.—Yus. I thort so. Just like you evac . . . . got persession of the eggs the week before larst, so that they could be sold at 'igher prices. Why don't we stop this ' ere profiteerin'?

Chairman.—Well, you know, Mr. Dogsbody the whole of the municipal staff have been giving much serious thought to the matter and have decided that nothing can be done.

Councillor Dogsbody.—Why?

Clerk.—Well, you see, sir. It's never been done before.

Councillor Dogsbody.—But why can't it be done now.

Clerk.—Because it would establish a precedent.

Councillor Dogsbody.—And wot abart it. Why shouldn't we establish a precedent? I dare say one of the members of the municipal orch . . . village band could soon learn to play it.

Chairman.—I don't think the Councillor quite understands. Precedents are dangerous things. We established one once and it went off .pop! Just like that! And since then we have followed the policy of not doing anything unless we can possibly help it.

Councillor Dogsbody.—And does he pay for the services we render him.

Chairman.—I must have notice of that question, but even if he does not, you must remember that in times like these everybody must help each other.

Councillor Dogsbody.—Yus, and these 'ere grocers seem to be helping themselves all right.

Clerk.—I've been looking up the matter in that well-known text book on municipal government entitled "One-thousand-and-one reasons for not doing anything," and there is clearly stated on the authority of Smith *v.* The Burpingham Town Council, P.D.Q. Div., L.T.R. Vol 67, cap. 5, that profiteering, so long as it is done in a gentlemanly manner is entirely unobjectionable. In his judgment, Mr. Justice Tumblebug delivers himself as follows:—

> Any council which does anything which it could possibly have avoided has bats in the belfry, and is thoroughly undeserving of the confidence reposed in it by the electors.

That, of course, gentlemen, is only an *obiter dictum* and not case law at present.

Councillor Dogsbody.—Wot we are talkin' abart is cases of sardines as I undersand it, so I move the Clerk is out of order referring to cases of law.

Chairman.—But the Councillor must understand the Council of Worpington-cum-slushpuddle must always be guided by precedents, even in er., unprecedented situations like this.

Councillor Dogsbody.—Very well then, how much profit is this 'ere Mr. Yu going' ter make out of ' is ' igher prices.

Chairman.—That, Mr. Councillor, is a most indelicate question. We as a Council could

"SAPAJOU" & "IN PARENTHESIS" OBSERVE THE WAR

GUNS vs. JACKS-IN-THE-BOX

"SAPAJOU" & "IN PARENTHESIS" OBSERVE THE WAR

never do anything so uncouth as to inquire into Mr. Yu's business.

Alderman Doolittle:—I think Mr. Chairman, that you and Councillor Dogsbody are, if I may say so, arguing at cross purposes. No one seems to think of the unfortunate plight of these poor sardines. Looking over the housing report the other day I noticed that a minimum space of 100 cubic feet is necessary for the individual. Now, I ask you, are our sardines given that much space? Let me assure members of the Council, that having opened a tin of sardines, I am in a position to state quite definitely that they are not. In fact the overcrowding of sardines is one of the questions which I had hoped to bring to the notice of the Council at no very distant date. Let me assure you, gentlemen, that if the matter were ever brought to the attention of the League of Nations, the name of Worpington-cum-slushpuddle would be mud. I think in the circumstances we should grant Mr. Yu's request and secure possession of the sardines in question, with a view to their early liberation. That Mr. Yu may make a somewhat higher profit on the subsequent sale is hardly a matter which we ought to go into now. The Council, I submit, must be motivated solely by er . . . motives of humanity.

Councillor Dogsbody.—Mr. Chairman and Councillors. Wot was it that Cardinal Wolsey said?

"Cromwell, I had not thought to shed a tear in all my misery,
But thou hast forced me, out of thine honest truth to play the woman."

The terrible plight of the tinned fish in question must rend the 'earts of all thinkin' men. I move that Mr. Yu is 'elped to get 'is sardines, and that a special grant be made to 'im, as an expression of this Council's 'igh opinion of the great, noble, and 'umane work 'e is 'adoin' of.

Exeunt omnes, Councillors singing "Here we go gathering nuts in May," as they leave the Council Chamber.

* * *

These Headings

JAPANESE WARSHIP
SAID SUNK OFF
KWANGCHOW HARBOUR

The captain of the vessel probably said "damn."

* * *

The Latest Developments

So, as we foretold,—or did we?—the wise guys, who could always tell when the "big push" was coming, have all proved to be wrong. There has been no such push. The Chinese retired from the positions they had held early, for the purpose of co-ordination and to get further away from the enemy's naval guns, while the Japanese just followed them. China certainly did not pull, and Japan didn't push.

What will happen to-day it is difficult to foresee. Of course being a Wednesday it is a half holiday but whether either side will recognize the fact is open to considerable doubt. If they don't we really think the bankers and brokers organizations should get busy on the subject. For, after all, fair's fair, as Miss Ipplethwick's auntie has always said.

It may be true that the Chinese have run, but not anywhere near as fast as the colour of some of the flags on display locally.

* * *

These War Stories

Some astonishing allegations are made in the statement issued by the Chinese delegation to the 18th meeting of the League of Nations. Thus:—

> During the last two months after engineering on the night of July 7 the Lukouchiao incident, Japan has sent an army of 2,500,000 men into North China. . . .
> Since the middle of August, Japan has mustered an army of more than 600,000 in the Shanghai-Woosung area. . .

Somebody is obviously telling tarradiddles, but, after all what are a few cyphers amongst friends?

* * *

A Quaint Practice

Announcing the gift of $10,000 to the police of Greater Shanghai in recognition of their excellent services during the present trouble, a "Central News" Service dispatch continues:—

> "In addition, the Government had dispatched Mr. Feng Yu-kun, chief of the Police Administration Department of the Ministry of Interior to Shanghai to 'comfort' the policemen."

Comforting a policeman is one of the most intricate jobs a government official can ever be called upon to perform. In London it is generally achieved by calling the man to be comforted before the Commissioner, who, after murmuring to him soothingly, gently strokes him behind the ears.

"SAPAJOU" & "IN PARENTHESIS" OBSERVE THE WAR

OUR BRAVE WOMEN-TYPISTS

"SAPAJOU" & "IN PARENTHESIS" OBSERVE THE WAR

Correspondence

DEAR I.P.

The following account taken from one of your esteemed evening contemporaries piques my curiosity:—

"Chinese amazons whose duty it is to "bolster the morale" of the Chinese troops are being used in the Woosung area . . . these women, some 500 of them, are in uniform and armed. . . None have been captured or found dead on the battlefield yet, the report having for its foundation the statement of a captured non-commission officer and the presence in Woosung of feminine underwear left behind during the retreat from that city."

Is it possible that the Chinese Army have forsaken Mah Jong for strip poker?

MAJOR OFFENSIVE.

The "non commission" officer has got me. As regards the feminine underwear, it looks like someone has made some sort of bloomer here.—I.P.

* * *

DEAR I.P.

What about the rumour that a couple of members of the Air Defence Company, S.V.C., were seen wending their way homeward the other day at 5 a.m.?

GENERAL NUISANCE.

Probably trying to "bolster" somebody's morals, or else members of the "Dawn Patrol."—I.P.

* * *

DEAR I.P.

What is this daily report about "Launching a fierce counter-offensive" that one reads in the papers? Does this refer to a boat or ship?

CORPORAL PUNISHMENT.

May be a ship—statesmanship. What a Hull of a question!—I.P.

* * *

Answers to Correspondents

Financial.—A wei wah cheque, is a strange war confection. If someone gives you a wei wah cheque, and you take it to a Chinese bank, the teller shouts "Wei!" with glee, to see you come in. If you try to get any money on the cheque, he merely says "Wah!" in derision. Some people spell it Hui-hua. But that's all hooey as far as we are concerned.

Camouflage

Much interest is caused out in the country by the sight of Chinese soldiers walking about with a branch of bamboo above their heads. And quite a few have come to us murmuring something about those two fellows Birnam Wood and Dunsinane, neither of whom are on our calling list, chiefly because their behaviour gave our dear old friend Macbeth the "woollies." Stranger still are the lorries decorated in the same way. This is said to be excellent camouflage designed to wreck the morale of the enemy. Aviators, looking down, and seeing a large sized bush prancing down the middle of a road, have been known to turn their machines round and head for home, swearing to keep off saké for the rest of their lives.

* * *

Right Every Time

It will be remembered that the large number of naval and military experts, who IN PARENTHESIS has succeeded in retaining, recently pointed out that when the two opposing forces were facing the same way one of them would be in retreat. How correct they were was proved on September 13. The discovery was not quite so novel as it appeared, though this was the first occasion it was made in connection with the present fracas. It is, of course, founded on that passage in the military textbook written by one Hannibal to the effect that: "It is better to look the enemy straight in the eye than to lay yourself open for a kick in the pants."

* * *

The Razzberry!

"The success of Japan's activities in China means only the abandonment by the Chinese leaders of the unfortunate anti-Japanism and the rejection of Communism," the Japanese Ambassador replied.

"The settlement of these two problems would bring about the co-operation of the two nations on an equal footing. Once this is clearly understood, there could be no room for raising the question as to the future of foreign trade or that of the present 'open door' policy of foreign trade in China."—"News Dispatch."

It is the "open door" policy, such as exists in Manchoukuo, which makes Japanese activities in China so absorbingly interesting to foreign traders.

* * *

War Reporting

The local correspondents swung into action splendidly on August 14, and now that the

"SAPAJOU" & "IN PARENTHESIS" OBSERVE THE WAR

SAFETY FIRST

"SAPAJOU" & "IN PARENTHESIS" OBSERVE THE WAR

London papers of the next day have come to hand it is possible to discover how terrible were the times through which Shanghai passed. Thus the Correspondent of the " Sunday Chronicle " " did his stuff " perfectly. Some of the choicer specimens follow:—

> " Shanghai is now struck by the havoc of a cruel and horrible war, I thought I had seen war at its worst in the last 20 years, but I have never seen anything like this ruthless devastation."
>
> " The roar of heavy artillery, anti-aircraft and machine-guns and rifle is deafening. With the crash of each falling bomb or collapsing building a fresh stream of panic stricken Chinese hurries into the European quarter and many are trampled underfoot in the mad rush."
>
> " During the bombing of the British owned Palace Hotel the Manager rushed downstairs shouting that there were six dead in one room."
>
> " Amid the hail of death from the skies a European woman on the Nanking Road was attempting to deliver her daughter of a child. There was nobody to help her but she went bravely on with her task regardless of peril."
>
> " The fate of China's millions lies in the hands of slight Soong Mayling, wife of Chiang Kai-shek, China's dictator."
>
> " When Chiang Kai-shek, Premier Dictator of China, left his capital at Nanking to meet the Japanese invaders, he left weeping, his chief adviser, Soong Mayling, his wife."
>
> " Soong Mayling has for long been the real brains behind the Chinese Government."
>
> " Chiang draws his strength and inspiration from his diminutive wife."
>
> " Many Britons, Europeans, and Americans spent the night in cellars."

It is very clear that the lad who wrote that has a vivid imagination and should go far, but how he found it all out in so short a time goodness only knows.

* * *

A Local Heading

RAIN DAMPENS WAR SPIRIT

Well, and what did you expect it to do?

* * *

The Back Seat

Now everybody in Europe has decided that they ought to have a crisis this Far Eastern schemozzle is attracting about as much attention as the bearded lady after a close shave.

* * *

Nature Note

" You know," one man remarked the other night, " This war is getting me down so much, that I often mistake a bird for an aeroplane."

If any of our readers experience the same difficulty they should remember that a bird flaps its wings. Aeroplanes found doing so are promptly disqualified.

* * *

What's in a Name?

From the " Japan Chronicle "—

> The Japanese Press notes that a large number of women are beginning to invade the ranks of workers in munitions plants as a result of the vacancies created by the departure of operatives on " grave affairs."

After all we prefer to call it an emergency: less macabre if you see what we mean.

* * *

Here's A New One

From the " Daily Mail " describing the arrival of the banknotes from Hongkong during the early days of the crisis:—

> " The money was landed on the Bund (Shanghai's Piccadilly) under cover of darkness."

Some people might liken the Bund to Petticoat Lane, though, of course, we prefer to think of it as Lombard Street.

* * *

The Discontented

There's no pleasing some people. During an air-raid the other evening the bar-flies were draped out of a window watching the proceedings with their courage in their hands, so to speak. The show was not quite up to the usual mark, with shooting poor and very erratic.

" Not so good this evening," remarked one hardened observer.

" Not so good?" queried another. " Why I think it's absolutely rotten."

Then we stepped in. " You know I don't think you ought to criticize so harshly. After all we're seeing the show for nothing."

* * *

The Food Situation

" Yes," remarked the old campaigner, reaching out for another. " No one need worry about the food situation if they would only do as I do. I haven't eaten since the trouble began."

TOO DEEPLY ROOTED

"Why, however do you manage?" asked the tenderfoot.

"Well, whenever I feel hungry I just sit apart and think. I think of my school-days, the old village church, of mother, and the first girl I ever loved. A lump comes in my throat, and all I have to do is swallow that." And he looked reflectively at his empty glass. We told this to Little Audrey and she laughed like one of those things which the Specialist wrote about.

* * *

Firm Action

> Special precautions were reported to have been taken by the Japanese Consular Police to prevent the spreading of the dread disease (cholera) into the Hongkew and Yangtszepoo districts, according to "Domei."

Cholera germs found in those areas will be promptly arrested and if found not to be in uniform will be taken out and shot immediately.

* * *

Away with the War

You know we do get fed up with this war every day, and wonder whether something cannot be done about it. The other day we were puzzling our minds to find something new to write about and the age-old question "Do shrimps make good mothers?" was recalled. You know, if Ike Newton had devoted more attention to this important question, instead of fooling round with the apple, who knows what advances might have been made in the study of natural history.

Anyhow the matter has been settled once and for all, for on the best of authority it is stated that some shrimps are called Oppossum shrimps from the fact that the female is provided with a ventral pouch or "marsupium," in which the eggs and young are carried.

It is satisfying to note that these interesting creatures frequent the seas around the English coast. One shudders to think what would happen if they were to be found around Australia. Fancy seeing an Australian throwing a kangaroo back into the water because it was too small!

* * *

Unkind

From a Hongkong contemporary:—

> And talking about trade interests in China there is also the story of the rat that deserted the ship that didn't sink.

Well, all we can say is that we haven't called anyone a rat *yet*.

From Hongkong

A man isn't a sardine because he lives in a tin house, writes Argus in the "S.C.M. Post,"—but it is apparently feared that a draughty stable may make a refugee a little hoarse.

* * *

All About Shanghai

A Shanghai newspaperman, who is comfortably settled in a Fleet Street office, has been contributing to the home papers articles about Shanghai. Not only did he tell his startled readers that there were 250,000 rickshaws in this city, but that he knew of bars in the place which had not been closed for fifty years. There is one thing about this war, incident or emergency, whichever you please, and that is that, before it has ended, we shall know quite a lot about this place which we never knew before.

* * *

Merely a Suggestion

The recent failures of the Chinese aircraft to make their before-dinner visitations to the Whangpoo are giving rise to a great deal of concern amongst the war fans. What they mean to say is, well, after all, if there is still some dispute as to who commands the air, couldn't some *modus vivendi* be arranged whereby each tide had control on alternate days. By some such means the truly amicable spirit in which these hostilities are being conducted might be perpetuated.

* * *

Just to Fool 'em

"Yes, my boy," remarked the old campaigner, leaning back and wiping the froth off his moustache. "You need never be afraid in war. Only the bullet that has your name and address on it will get you."

"Then it ought to be easy to come through safely," we remarked guilelessly.

"How do you mean."

"Why, just change house, and the bullet won't know anything about it."

* * *

More Comfort

Tokyo, Sept. 16.

> Six master sword-makers—all members of the Dai-Nippon Sword Dealers' Association—left here this afternoon for China to comfort Japanese soldiers.
>
> During their tour of North China and Shanghai, the members of the party will mend and sharpen military swords

"SAPAJOU" & "IN PARENTHESIS" OBSERVE THE WAR

AS OTHERS SEE US

"SAPAJOU" & "IN PARENTHESIS" OBSERVE THE WAR

Each, on his departure to-day, wore a special uniform and carried a Japanese sword.—"Domei."

It is so comforting to have one's sword sharpened for one.

* * *

Coming Retribution

Asks an advertisement :—

ARE YOU BORED

with the tedious solitude which is occasioned by your family's absence?

The answer seems to be in the negative. Some men we know are having the time of their lives, and will continue to do so when wives get to know all about it.

* * *

To-day's Great Question

Have you a little wei-wah in your home? If not, why not.

The wei-wah is not to be mistaken for the wah-wah. The latter is a perfectly good monkey. The former is just monkeying about.

* * *

Great News

Motion picture producers in Hollywood are speeding up production in order to capitalize on the Sino-Japanese hostilities. Pictures in preparation include "North of Shanghai," "Daughter of Shanghai," "West of Shanghai," and "Shanghai Deadline."

Oh boy! Oh boy! Oh boy! aren't we getting a lot of publicity? It is to be hoped that these pictures reach Shanghai so that we can see how the Hollywood producer fancies Shanghai behaves itself under shot and shell. "Shanghai Deadline," of course, should deal with newspaper men, and let us inform you the way those boys are sticking to their jobs is nobody's business,— except theirs.

* * *

These Military Dicta

It was a bright lad who remarked that an army marches on its stomach, but we have never yet seen a military tummy soled and heeled.

Then there was another cove who stated that Waterloo was won on the playing fields of Eton. It is remarks like this that make the Borstal boys class conscious.

And how about every soldier carrying a field marshal's baton in his knapsack, when all a good soldier asks for now is a really useful entrenching tool?

Someone Has Blundered

Heading in a local paper :—

JAPANESE CLAIM ADVANCE HERE IN LIUHONG SECTOR; CHINESE DECLARE LOTION AREA RE-TAKEN

Lotion as before, we gather.

* * *

Oh, Very Terse

Clerk coming into the taipan's office on the Bund, while a "hate" was proceeding on the Whangpoo, with a telegram from his wife, in Hongkong, instructing him to store her furs and jewellery :—

"What do you think, sir, would be a safe place to store them?"

"The Idzumo," was the swift reply.

* * *

How True

"While deploring the news of its (the Civic Centre) damage, he (Gen. Wu Teh-chen) praised the behaviour of the Chinese people in Shanghai during the present crisis, fully endorsing the statement of the present Mayor, Mr. O. K. Yui, that "the enemy will not be there long."—"Reuters Pacific Service."

The "enemy" is in astonishing agreement with this forecast, and the only difference in ideas which appears to exist is as to the direction in which the next move is to be made.

* * *

Miaow!

The Japanese spokesman :—

It is customary for the Chinese to claim a major victory just before a general retreat so it is expected that they will soon retire from the Lotien area.

Now we think this is definitely unkind. Only the day before a Chinese spokesman conceded the capture of Kiangwan Race Course to the Japanese, while the latter insisted that the Chinese held it. Unless this fracas can be conducted with politeness all round, it had better be called off.

* * *

The Unexpected

BERLIN, Sept. 17.—The "Algemeine Zeitung" yesterday published an article by the retired General Karl Held, in which he stated that China's tenacious resistance for the last six weeks around

EMERGENCY MILLINERY

"SAPAJOU" & "IN PARENTHESIS" OBSERVE THE WAR

Shanghai, Peiping and Tientsin had surprised Europe.

Yeah! And it wasn't only Europe that was surprised!

* * *

Some Bombing

Nanking, Sept. 13.

In reprisal for what is considered the illegal blockade of the China coast, the Chinese air-force carried out a successful raid on Japanese naval ships in the region of Kwangchow Bay at ten o'clock this morning. The attack was carefully planned and came as a surprise to the enemy. *Several bombs were dropped and each is reported to have struck its mark with the result that there were numerous explosions which could be heard for miles around.* Flames rising high into the sky from one of the ships gave evidence of the fact that it was badly hit and a short while later she was seen to sink. All of the planes sent out returned safely to their base—"Central News."

This 100 per cent effective air-bombing just shows what the Chinese aviators can do when they are really on their mettle.

* * *

Diplomacy

A determined attempt is being made by Japan to regain international goodwill. One of the strongest cards played up to the present is to be found in the suggestion that when they have won whatever is on at present, one of the terms of peace will be that China shall revert to the 5 per cent *ad valorem* tariff. With the consequent reduction in the price of liquor it is expected that a better feeling will be induced all round.

* * *

Now We Know

Mr. Carl Crow, who recently wrote something about 400,000,000 customers, and as an advertising man may be expected to be fully conversant with political and military probabilities, has declared in an interview given in Seattle:—

"China is sure to hold out for two years fighting a defensive battle. By that time Japan will have been licked"

Prophecy in connection with military matters is at all times a risky business. As things look at present especially in the North, it would seem that the Chinese are winning all along the line, showing a much finer turn of speed.

And We Like

The story of the householder who returned into Hongkew to secure some of his belongings and found a notice from a public utility company, which shall be nameless, informing him that unless he paid his bill by a certain date his electricity would be cut off. He isn't half laughing!

* * *

Ain't Nature Grand?

A "Personal" advertisement.—

"Lonely Briton seeks companionship of lady, any nationality, of independent means, willing to travel, and assist financially in profitable business. Reply particulars. Strictly, confidential."

The position she would occupy, of course, would be that of an active, sleeping partner.

* * *

The Real McKay!

Machine-gunners capable of holding their weapons down to three shots every firing and keeping it up at regular intervals are considered experts of the highest degree.

Says a contemporary writing of the new gunners placed in Pootung. The trick of only firing three shots in a burst is designed to prevent enemy aviators ascertaining where the machine-guns are situated. It is obvious that if they fire a stream of bullets all the aviator has to do is to look down the stream to find where the gun is hidden. Simple, my dear Watson.

* * *

Making Our Flesh Creep

The Sydney "Sun" has done the Shanghai story proud, and seeing its issue of August 16, In Parenthesis is convinced that Shanghai has not yet really understood what happened to it on Black Saturday. The paper in question publishes a picture of the Bund. In it the artist has placed all the products of his fertile imagination. The Shanghai Club will be surprised to know that it went up in flames, the Hongkong & Shanghai Bank dome did a sort of pyrotechnic act, the "North-China Daily News" suffered in such good company as did also Jardine, Matheson & Co. We have known for years that we have been dead from the neck up, but the completeness of our demise has come as an appalling shock. We shall be calling very shortly to collect our insurance money.

"SAPAJOU" & "IN PARENTHESIS" OBSERVE THE WAR

IN FELL COLLABORATION

"SAPAJOU" & "IN PARENTHESIS" OBSERVE THE WAR

This Horrible War

The Chinese Embassy spokesman has been telling the tale in Washington, judging from a message carried by the United Press :—

"According to the spokesman, It was also understood the Japanese were reportedly contemplating landing on the Shanghai Bund for the purpose of attacking Nantao."

One of these days someone will be telling the truth about the local situation. Actually, if the Japanese do land on the Bund it is expected that some people will be very hurt about it.

* * *

Military Note

This rainy weather has caught both sides completely unawares. IN PARENTHESIS learns on the best authority that the two high commands have reported to their governments that unless the men are immediately equipped with bathing costumes the present enjoyable little shindy will have to be completely abandoned.

* * *

A Bit 'ard.

Every sympathy will be felt with the man recently convicted and given a suspended sentence in the U.S. Court, who has now been ordered to leave China or undergo the prescribed imprisonment. It's a bit 'ard to be sent away from Shanghai just now.

* * *

How Very Unkind

It is reported that the air-raids on Shanghai on Saturday were arranged to mark the humiliation day celebrating the Manchurian incident in 1932. The bombing of neutral property was a very effective way of "taking it out of" the enemy.

* * *

Warning

IN PARENTHESIS wishes to warn his readers that he may have to suspend this here war for a few days. A tour of Shanghai streets showed that the emergency emplacements were losing their pristine neatness, and it will be necessary to launder the sandbags before we can proceed any further.

* * *

Descriptive

During the air-raid on Saturday evening we encountered the Old Campaigner.

"And how do you feel to-day?" we asked.

"Low," was the reply. "As low as a duck's tail and shaking twice as fast."

* * *

A Literary

Monday morning's cannonading reminded us of the passage in the poem, "There was a sound of devilry by night" in which the poet remarks, so rightly, if you remember :—" It is, it is the cannon's opening roar."

You all know the poem we refer to. One verse ends "They called him little Jim," and another "Don't go down the mine, Daddy."

* * *

A Bit Unkind

One of the first U.S. Marine officers to land is reported to have remarked :—

"Well it's the same old business again, defending Soochow Creek."

He should be made to understand that we Shanghailanders are proud of the Creek. It may not look up to much, but we must always think of the odoriferous cargoes its mercantile marine carries on its gleaming buzzum.

* * *

A Discrepancy

There seems to be a slight difference of opinion between Admiral Hasegawa and the Japanese official spokesman :—

The Admiral.—the Commander-in-Chief of the Third Fleet of H.I.J.M's Navy is constrained earnestly to advise such officials and residents as are living in and around Nanking to take adequate measures for voluntarily moving into areas of greater safety.

The Japanese spokesman.—

The objectives of the Japanese air force are not Embassies or the residence of high Chinese officials. We aim at military establishments and bases of military operations

Well, there you are. Having paid no money you are entitled to a free choice of which you believe.

* * *

That Rose

The one main thing upon which military spokesmen for both sides seem to agree is that the Japanese are bringing in a great deal of military equipment,

TOUJOUR LA POLITESSE!

The Chinese state, for instance, that the Japanese are digging in with heavy trench mortars in several positions, and frequent mention is made of tanks and light artillery.

We've heard a spade called a sanguinary shovel, but this is quite the first time we have heard it spoken of as a trench mortar.

* * *

Then There's the Story

Of the Sergeant Major who tried to explain to the Colonel, in the most restrained language possible, the hardship of being expected to form fours with only three men.

* * *

These Astrologers

Edward Lyndoe, of "The People," is bent on making the flesh creep of the Japanese :—

> It is a matter of years since I told you that should the Japanese enter Peking there would follow a national collapse. I remind you of this old prophecy because the next few weeks mark the beginning of an extraordinary run of ill-luck for Japan, in spite of relatively unimportant military successes.
>
> A big dispute with America is on the way for Tokyo, and there are certain indications of an attack launched by Russia. Anyway, I have always insisted that the Far East was the world's danger-zone—not the West. It will not be long before Britain and the U.S.A. stage a definite link-up covering the affected areas, and I expect a big "naval demonstration."

Of course, if all this happens, and the stars are such undependable factors in international politics, it looks as though Japan is going to get it where the chicken got the axe.

* * *

My Gawd!

A reader sends us the following :—

> "You mentioned the other day that the war might have to be called off for a few days as sandbags were out of repair owing to the heavy rain. I noticed this morning, at the entrance to the Embankment Building, that the sandbags there are shooting out sprouts of green. As the Welch Fusiliers have been in the building for two or three weeks are they springing leeks?"

It's things like this that are busily turning our hair gray and almost sending us back to honest journalism again.

* * *

The Nervy "Nippo"

A local editor takes a heavy swipe at a local Japanese contemporary :—

> NIPPO'S NERVE
>
> In some respects we are no admirer of the Shanghai "Nippo," but we like its nerve. This Japanese organ calls for gratitude, "not for complaints and abuse, or for demands for a free return of foreigners to their former homes," in connection with the recent access given foreigners to their property in the northern Settlement areas, we feel, is a trifle too thick.

Seems to us there is too much "barracking" from the ringside seats.

* * *

Coo!

From a local weekly :—

> Not the least of the funny things about this war is the fact that while the Eve Post without argument cops the laurels for timely, accurate, extensive war-news publishing, the Snooze gets the silver shaving mug for cornering the local humour market. This "In Parenthesis" column is getting to be something to really write home about.

IN PARENTHESIS blushes and likewise bows, but with all the diffidence in the world, would suggest that, perhaps, the editor of the paper in question is a better judge of humour than of news.

* * *

Come to Hongkong

Quite a number of people have written to Shanghai complaining of conditions in Laichikok Jail, to which Shanghai refugees have been transferred from the Jockey Club buildings in Happy Valley.

Really, we are completely at a loss to understand the ingratitude of some people. Here they are removed to quieter quarters where their sleep shall not be disturbed by the early morning training gallops for the Autumn Meeting, and all they do is to grouse about it!

CUSTODIAN:—WELL, IT'S A NEW ONE ON ME!

"SAPAJOU" & "IN PARENTHESIS" OBSERVE THE WAR

AERIAL AND NAUTICAL

Volume 2

SHANGHAI'S SCHEMOZZLE

2nd Spasm

by

SAPAJOU

with

R. T. PEYTON-GRIFFIN

("In Parenthesis")

Reprinted from Cartoons and " In
Parenthesis " which have appeared in
the North-China Daily News from
September 28, 1937

SHANGHAI
PRINTED AT THE OFFICE OF THE NORTH-CHINA DAILY NEWS & HERALD, LTD
1938

FOREWORD

SAPAJOU AND IN PARENTHESIS present their second spasm of the Shanghai Schemozzle in the hope that readers will obtain as much enjoyment from perusing it as they have had in its compilation.

The two of them have been perfect nuisances around the office, stalking about with fixed eyes and doleful countenances, thinking of something new to pull on the long-suffering public. The more successful Sapajou was the gloomier he would look, while the self-satisfaction of In Parenthesis was generally betrayed by his unfortunate habit of humming the sadder strains from the hymnology. That wouldn't have been so bad, if the refrain had not occasionally been taken up by the News Editor, who had also been a choirboy in his dim and murky past,—why is it that choirboys and clergymen's daughters so often go wrong?

But be that as it may, Sap and Ip have disregarded any inconvenience they may have put their colleagues to, and have gone their way as unrepentantly as ever.

Both of them say, though, that if Shanghai never has another schemozzle it will, even then, be much too soon.

SEEING IT THROUGH

"SAPAJOU" & "IN PARENTHESIS" OBSERVE THE WAR

Playing Safe?

One of the vernacular papers reports that the Shanghai Bar Association, which in normal times actively supports all movements for the abolition of extraterritoriality, has made a number of recommendations to the Government. It is understood, however, that immediate rendition of the Foreign Settlement and French Concession is not one of them.

* * *

Our Air Experts

"The craft had just taken off and was attempting to bank when the Nipponese pilot lost control and came down. It was a drop of about 800 feet, and whether the plane was badly damaged or not could not be ascertained."

Planes dropping a mere 800 feet do not as a rule get badly damaged. They merely bounce.

* * *

The Co-optimists

"If only the invaders would stop and seriously ask themselves the question. For what purpose are we fighting? and then weigh carefully the cost against the possible gain, we might hope for a return to sanity and peace, with prospect of prosperity in the distance."

It is quite time the Japanese did ask themselves the question seriously. Up to the present they seem to have been regarding the whole matter as a huge joke.

* * *

Gloomy Outlook

From Mr. C. C. Wong's letter to "The Times":—

"Peace-loving nations must remember what President Lincoln said: "unless we hang together we shall be hanged separately."

Huh! Seems a hanging job either way.

* * *

The Governing Classes

Writes a reader in yesterday's correspondence columns:—

"It is common knowledge that vast fortunes have been acquired in recent times by the governing classes."

In Parenthesis sincerely hopes that in the above sentence there is no suggestion of "squeeze," though singularly enough it is a fact that very substantial sums have been made by *buying* munitions.

* * *

A Safe Bet

BIG OFFENSIVE
SAID IN OFFING

This particular caption will stand good for a few days more.

* * *

New Social Distinction

Irate Lady:—I beg your pardon. I was an *evacuee*, not a refugee.

* * *

This Quaint World

From a letter in yesterday's issue:—

Resistance at the present time will not benefit the Chinese people, active intervention by the Soviets might aid China to a great extent, but at what a cost in concessions and territory which the Soviets will later claim?

The "Nichi Nichi's" correspondent at Paotingfu predicts that an autonomous federation of the five provinces in North China—Hopei, Shantung, Shansi, Suiyuan and Charhar—will be organized following the successful termination of Japanese military operations. Seems to us the less said about the cost to China in concessions and territory at the present moment the better, in this wonderful game of grab.

* * *

The Charmed Life

Now that attempts to "get" the Idzumo from the air and in the water have failed, it seems that the only method left untried is harpooning.

* * *

Descriptive Writers Again

No one yet has perpetrated the "great diapason of war," though one or two of them have been toying with the symphony idea.

* * *

We Like the Story

Of the Japanese aviators who mistook dairy cows for cavalry horses and wiped them out with machine-guns and bombs.

It reminds us of little Gwendoline, who came home one day and told her mother she had been attacked in the park by a great big lion.

"SAPAJOU" & "IN PARENTHESIS" OBSERVE THE WAR

MODERN LIMITATIONS

"Now," said mother, "You're a naughty girl. You must go straight to your bedroom and tell all your naughtiness to your guardian angel."

The little girl did so, and later returned with a satisfied look on her face.

"Did you do what I told you?" asked the mother, "and tell your guardian angel all about it."

"Yes, mamma, I did, and all he said was 'Please don't mention it, Miss Gwendoline, I've often mistaken those big yellow dogs for lions myself.'"

* * *

The War is Spreading

Even to the vitamins, for we read in a local contemporary, on excellent medical authority that

"Most people know that the vitamins in general are labelled A,B,C,D, and E, and that B is sometimes called F, and E, and that B is sometimes called F, and G.

The situation at the most is said not to be greatly strained, but tension is expected to increase unless something is done about it.

* * *

Success

Keep an eye on international developments. They are moving fast. In piling up world-wide public opinion for China, Japan is proving China's best friend!

All of which seems to show that Japan's friendly overtures to China are succeeding all along the line.

* * *

The Newer Warfare

As a Chinese military observer sums up the situation, the Japanese will obviously make a desperate attempt to punctuate the Chinese lines at two points, Kiangwan in the south and Lotien in the north.

Punctuating a defence is a very delicate military operation, performed with an acupunctuator!

* * *

A Protest

We admit that a cruiser belonging to a certain nation is a bit of an eyesore to another certain nation, but really it's a bit thick to call her the Eczema.

Answers to Correspondents

Enquirer:—A military observer is one who observes military operations and then comes back and makes observations to the Press. A spokesman is one who says a lot but really tells little.

* * *

A Gloomy Forecast

From an editorial in a local contemporary:—

As noted students of Chinese history, the Japanese authorities must be able to recall that the founders of the Yuan Dynasty spent over 30 years to suppress "bandits" who were really Chinese patriots refusing to accept an alien rule, and an equal period to compose differences among the descendants of the conqueror himself.

If that means that the writer anticipates that the Chinese and Japanese are to continue mucking about like they are now for the next sixty years, we don't like the prospect at all.

* * *

Prognostication

To-day being Saturday, the day on which the Chinese always have control of the air, if you get what we mean, it is possible that there will be an air raid to-night. These Saturday bombings are the result of a cleverly thought out plan to prevent the Japanese troops from having their weekly bath, a particularly effective piece of frightfulness, about which it is expected Japan will appeal to the League of Nations.

* * *

Discomforting

Mr. Isumo—that name again,—Japanese Consul-General at Geneva, thinks at the moment it is best to let things take their course. In any event, he added, the intervention of a third party would be liable to cause complications.

Thus, for example, supposing Russia were to intervene matters would become complicated indeed. All that Japan wants in China is a fair field and no favour, but more especially the field.

* * *

Something Wrong

While we were busy writing this, yesterday morning, the strains of a well-known Christmas carol came in through the window. The song was most inappropriate because over in Chapei the Japanese aeroplanes *were* raising 'ell.

WITH APOLOGIES TO PHIL MAY

Lunatic (suddenly popping his head over wall) :—" What are you doing there ? "
Combatants :—" Fighting "   *Lunatic* :—" Anybody beaten yet ? "   *Combatants* :—" No."
Lunatic :—" How long have you been at it ? "   *Combatants* :—" Six weeks."
Lunatic :—" *COME INSIDE !* "

"SAPAJOU" & "IN PARENTHESIS" OBSERVE THE WAR

The Dear Old S.M.C.

Did you notice on Sunday that the Municipal Council announced that it had discovered profiteering? In Parenthesis found that out shortly after the outbreak of the what-is-it, but then the Council probably thought he was merely "seeing things."

* * *

Says A Local Advertiser

BE NONCHALANT!

When the conflict is at its height... be nonchalant. Appear cool and unconcerned is a suit superbly tailored by...

What, and have it all mucked up by the combatants?

* * *

Fashion Note

WAR BECOMES GENERAL

reports a weekly magazine.

It has even been known to suit some corporals.

* * *

Why?

Reports that peace talks had taken place recently in Shanghai were denied yesterday by the Chinese spokesman. No Chinese authorities had initiated such negotiations, he added, and if they had been started by the Japanese he was not aware of them.

Why should there be any peace when both sides are winning so splendidly?

* * *

So Apt

HAN FU-CHU

STILL SAID

ON FENCE

In other words a mugwump. You know, his mug on one side and his wump on the other.

* * *

Military Note

Judging from some of the anti-aircraft firing we have seen in the Whangpoo recently it would seem that Chinese aeroplanes come from all directions at once. Of course, there is no reason why that shouldn't be done, but it's a little difficult for one machine to do it.

Sound Advice

"Britain should not dash in and join other nations in too great a hurry to try and compel these people to fall apart."

In other words it's a poor boob who tries to prevent two loving friends from clinching, if they want to.

* * *

Where Are We Now?

The Japanese Navy denies attacking and sinking Chinese fishing junks, but claims that armed junks have been attacking it. This frightfulness on the part of the Chinese fishing fleet is most strongly to be deprecated.

* * *

In a Nutshell

A local editor writes:—

"The Chinese defender... knows not what it is to fear, since Japanese shells and bombs sends one equally to perdition, whether one takes it manfully or shivering in one's shoes. And until the invader comes out of his trench to give combat, the defender may as well while away the hours by fiddling on his *Hu-ch'in* or playing mahjongg."

In case anyone doesn't know it a *Hu-ch'in* appears to be some sort of fiddle.

* * *

Point of Etiquette

A heading:—

GHOST OF HANNIBAL

VISITS SHANGHAI

The late lamented Carthaginian gentleman should, of course, be referred to as "Mr. Hannibal."

* * *

For Brighter Wars

Quite one of the newest ideas in sandbag emplacements is the one in Avenue Edward VII which was recently concreted over. The inside has now been painted a choice crushed strawberry colour. When it has been pointed up with a little cream coloured trimming the whole effect will be quite too-too for words.

* * *

So Now We Know

According to the spokesman of the Japanese Foreign Office, Japan wants neither to make China solely dependent on her nor to take any part of China's territory.

THE SWORD OF DAMOCLES

All that China has to do, therefore, to make Tokyo really angry is to offer to surrender the five northern provinces, which, at great expense, Japan is saving for China.

* * *

Well, well, well!

Those sub-editors again:—
SUB-COMMITTEE OF 13
MOLLS OVER CHINESE
JAPANESE VIEWS

We've heard the League of Nations called a lot of things in the past, but never before have we heard of the delegates being spoken of as molls.

* * *

Strictly True

SUB-COMMITTEE
SEEKS FACTS ON
CHINA DISPUTE.

Dozens of newspapermen listening to the different spokesmen daily are even now only sure of one thing and that is that something is up.

* * *

This Contagious War

Things are going from bad to worse and assault and battery seem to be the order of the day, as witness this caption:—
HART-BAKER
STRIKES FORM
IN FRIENDLY

* * *

Says a Contemporary

The Rotary Club was founded by a coal dealer, a merchant tailor, a lawyer and a mining operator.

Well, why bring that up at a time like this?

* * *

Trade Note

An advertiser is offering sandbags for hire. There is now no reason whatever why you shouldn't have a little sandbag in your home. It's quite likely, though, that some enterprising firm will soon offer sandbags on the hire purchase system. We can't think of anybody nowadays who wouldn't like to own a nice real sandbag.

The Manila Refugees

"And everybody is helping out everybody," Mrs. Howes said—in an interview.—"Before I came down, I had to help a mother heat up the flat iron with which to iron some diapers."

There is quite an art in helping to make a flat iron hot.

* * *

Oh No!

Junius Secundus doesn't half take a swipe at all the prominent Chinese who have recently been making money:—

"The $200,000 which the Refugee Committee had indicated as necessary for its work, could have been collected from Chinese sources within a day considering the ample means available in that direction. Before our Chinese friends can expect sacrifices and assistance from foreign sympathizers they must show the way in a substantial manner themselves."

Perhaps the foreigners would do better for themselves by following the example which has already been set.

* * *

Yesterday Afternoon

Gwendoline, the dear child, dropped in yesterday afternoon, just as we were finishing "copy" for this column.

"Why the wrinkled brow, I.P., the dull careworn look in the eye, the brooding of melancholy?"

"I wish you wouldn't come butting in here during office hours. A regular pest, that's what you are. What do you want now?"

"I was wondering if you could come and take me out for tea."

"Look here my child, do you realize that there's a war on, and the public wants to know all about it?"

"Do you think it is necessary that they should? They can hear the bombing and shelling. For the life of me I don't see why they should want to read about it, with all those unpronounceable names, and that sort of thing. And, anyhow, what does it matter if one side or the other is being pushed back? It all sounds so terribly rude to me, if you understand what I mean."

"Well, war is rude anyhow."

"Very well, if war is rude, I don't think people ought to read about it. Come and take me out to tea."

"SAPAJOU" & "IN PARENTHESIS" OBSERVE THE WAR

A WARNING TO THE UNWARY

(*And thus, with a scant three inches to go, the typewriter is hushed, and the printers allowed to get their fell work in.*)

* * *

A Bitter Blow

> CITY RUNS OUT OF
> COCA-COLA

That's nothing. In one of the haunts which we frequent they have run out of our particular brand of joy-juice. We're not complaining, but if something isn't done about it, nothing will be.

* * *

The Softies

From a news item :—

> A score of sailors from the . . . were heard to complain loudly that the frequent shelling of Pootung by Japanese warships interfered with their sleep.

We know one man who has become so hardened now that when everything is quiet, he keeps his boy up all night slamming a door so that he can get a little rest.

* * *

Comic Interlude

Says Mr. Frederick L. Kerran, British Labour Leader, according to a contemporary :—

> "I believe that the report as to the attitude of the British Government to the boycott must not be read as it appears on the surface. The British have a very clever ruling class and it is just possible that the reported reluctance of the Government to endorse the boycott may just mean the opposite of what it says."

Boiled down to plain English this means that the British Government is composed of terminological inexactitudinarians, and that the making of wholly veracious statements is the exclusive monopoly of the Labour Party.

* * *

High Praise

This war is regaining some of the old-fashioned courtesy again. Reporting last Friday night's air-raids by the Chinese, a contemporary paid the Japanese a high compliment :—

> "The show displayed by the Japanese was one of the best they have furnished to date. While the anti-aircraft fire was not so heavy as it was two weeks ago, this evening when the Chinese raiders visited the lower Yangtszepoo area and set several fires, new searchlights were brought into use."

The interchange of delicate compliments like this is expected to make this war a much more pleasurable event.

* * *

Another Name

From a local contemporary :—

> The Chinese have found a word for this in terming the Shanghai hostilities as a "saw-saw" war, with especial reference to the frequent exchange of minor positions between the contending parties. The idea seems to be to suggest a carpenter hard at work drawing his saw back and forth.

Well, the Chinese might call it a saw-saw war, and the Japanese deny that it is a war at all, while we are convinced that it is just a damned nuisance. So there!

* * *

How True?

> Although Tientsin is one centre of Sino-Japanese hostilities, the northern port is apparently losing no time in returning to normalcy. The Tientsin Grammar School, it is reported, re-opened for the autumn term on September 9 with an enrolment of 288 pupils, of whom 144 are boys and a like number girls.

There is an overwhelming amount of accuracy in the above mathematical statement.

* * *

Our War Review

This being the end of the seventh week of the local what-is-it? IN PARENTHESIS'S experts are reporting on the situation. They find that it has developed most interestingly. For instance the long heralded big push has been in operation on both sides since Jupiter Pluvius withdrew from the scene of action and reduced the number of contestants to the original two. Each side during the last week has been busy repelling the advances of the other and the efficiency with which this manœuvre has been carried out has resulted in the fact that both parties are very much where they were when they started. The situation may now be said to be static,—hydro- or ec- as the case might be.

"SAPAJOU" & "IN PARENTHESIS" OBSERVE THE WAR

WATCH YOUR STEP, GUV'NOR!

"SAPAJOU" & "IN PARENTHESIS" OBSERVE THE WAR

Startling News

From a statement issued by the Japanese Embassy in London:—

> As Japanese submarines are strictly forbidden to attack merchantmen, junks, etc., and as no Japanese submarine is operating in the locality, it is absolutely impossible that any attack such as is alleged to have been made, could have occurred.

It is now suspected that one of those submarines which formerly had been operating in the Mediterranean must have been responsible.

* * *

Very Likely True

You know, we like that story about the use by the Japanese of a large number of bulls to lead an attack on Chinese lines. The only difficulty we had was in discovering where the Japanese got the bulls from. That, however, has been completely solved. The Chinese farmers in the area when they evacuated left the bulls behind because they thought the animals might amuse the Chinese soldiers fighting for their country. Then when the Chinese troops made the strategic retreat they left the bulls behind out of sheer hospitality, believing that the Japanese soldiers would like a little beef on the hoof for their sukiyaki. Reports vary as to whether the animals so used were bulls or cows. This is quite peculiar for we understand there is considerable difference between the two.

* * *

Our Transport Companies

From a letter in Saturday's issue:—

> "All boiled down the basic cause of the dissatisfaction appears to be the undoubted fact that rates of cargo transportation have for many years been too low to be profitable, except perhaps to the native driver owners who are for the time being out of the market."

The picture which the above presents is of the foreign transport companies carrying on their business for years at a loss and doing it very enthusiastically—chronic philanthrophists so to speak.

* * *

The Situation

Expert observers summing up the situation as it has recently developed find that the Japanese in some sectors of the line have advanced three kilometres between September 14 and October 4. If this rate of progress is continued they may be expected to get somewhere at some time or other, or possibly even before.

Of course if either side would only realize when it was beaten one or the other would gain a decisive victory. Personally, we think it ought to be called a draw with no opportunity afforded for a replay.

* * *

Archbishop's Silence

It is reported that the Archbishop of Canterbury is maintaining silence with regard to the protest of the Anglican Bishop of South Tokyo against the former presiding over a meeting to protest against the Japanese air-raids over China.

Considering how vocal the Archbishop has been of late it is hoped that this act of self-denial will not impose too great a strain on him.

* * *

"Hell Let Loose"

Under the above caption the editor of the "Hongkong Daily Press" lets himself go as follows:—

> "For almost thirty years Japan has thieved, pillaged and murdered in the implementing of her general plan for peaceful settlement of Sino-Japanese problems. The employment of that gracious word "peaceful" in connection with Japan's policy of unadulterated rapacity is a hollow mockery sufficient to make even a cynic physically as well as morally sick.

You know when we read stuff like that we begin to realize that we really do get value for our money in the daily newspaper.

* * *

Not So Good

What each opponent thinks of the other in this local what-you-may-call-it is amply shown in these excerpts taken from recent Chinese and Japanese reports:—

The Chinese say:—

> The gallantry and bravery as displayed by their fathers during the Russo-Japanese War are no longer the traits of the Japanese soldiers of to-day, declared a foreign military observer in Nanking.

STILL FAR AWAY

And the Japanese say:—

> As the Chinese forces from the Lotien-Liuhong sector retreat towards Kiating and their second line of defences, from the way that military supplies are being left behind it is thought that the morale of the soldiers must be going down rapidly.

In other words neither side thinks much of the other.

* * *

The Sentimentalists

Judging from some of the sentiments expressed in the correspondence columns, there are some enthusiasts who would embark upon another war in the sacred interests of peace.

* * *

And then

There's another of those correspondents who appears to think that Japanese bombing behaviour is "not cricket." The sooner some people begin to understand that war never was, they will have a better perception of what it really is.

* * *

This Very Sad World

> Although definite information is still lacking regarding the true state of affairs it is reliably reported that harmony is sadly missing among Manchoukuo officials and Japanese advisers.

In other words Manchoukuo would much rather fiddle on the *Hu-ch'in* than strum on the *samisen*.

* * *

Merely a Suggestion

In view of all that has happened, isn't it just about time someone protested against the bombing of open cities in Spain?

* * *

Natural History Note

There's quite a lot of misinformation in the average newspaper heading, thus:—

> W. J. MONK DECIDES HAGGIS
> DISCARDED BAGPIPE

This, of course, is all wrong: the haggis never had a bagpipe.

A Protest

In a very kindly reference to the result of Sapajou and ourself gambolling on the green during this "Much Ado About Nothing," a local contemporary dealing with In PARENTHESIS writes:—

> "He can be devastatingly cynical as well as broadly funny."

If this reference to breadth concerns our personal dimensions it is greatly to be deplored. As for being cynical, we have always considered ourself a "child of light."

* * *

A Solution at Hand

Reports the United Press:—

> Tokyo, Oct. 5.
> Putting Japan on an even fuller basis of preparedness, the Government to-day published a draft list of prohibited or restricted imports and exports. . . . .
> The list was divided into three sections: firstly, prohibited exports, chiefly munitions, which were not detailed. . . . .

Now if Japan will only prohibit the export of munitions to China this present goodness-knows-what-it-is would soon come to an end.

* * *

Moscow Happy

A news dispatch from Moscow says:—

> Russia is very optimistic with regard to the war in China, believing that the Japanese invaders will soon be confronted with untold difficulties. Meanwhile, as a result of the heroic resistance put up by the brave Chinese soldiers, a good part of the Japanese troops will be kept too busy to turn their attention to anything else. Russia's military position in the Far East, therefore, will be considerably improved.

From what we see of it someone seems to be fighting somebody else's battle.

* * *

A Complaint

In Parenthesis has a very definite complaint to make against the Chinese authorities. Until Tuesday the starting time for air-raids was 6.35 p.m. precisely, and Friday or Saturday generally the evenings chosen. The departure from schedule has seriously interfered with certain financial manipulations. In fact on Tuesday he lost. If this sort of thing continues he will have to boycott these air-raids.

"SAPAJOU" & "IN PARENTHESIS" OBSERVE THE WAR

THE GARDEN OF (MR.) EDEN

"SAPAJOU" & "IN PARENTHESIS" OBSERVE THE WAR

It's All Wrong

" This is a heck of a war," one visiting newsman complained, " we came here to get news and all we get is bedtime stories at press conferences."

Statements like this are apt to confuse the minds of those endeavouring to understand the situation. It has been said time out of number that this is not a war, so how the heck can it be a heck of a one?

* * *

Take Care, Charlie!

It is reported that the famous Charlie Chan, who likes to conduct his campaigns single-handed, has captured the roof of the Tumble Inn as his vantage point. It is sincerely hoped he will take every precaution to see that he doesn't tumble off.

* * *

Strong Arm Methods

Dr. Koo vigorously insisted on a formal condemnation of Japanese aggression by the committee.

If satisfaction were not granted, he should refuse to accept the credit of Swiss Frs. 2,000,000 given by the League for action against epidemics in China.—*Petition by Chinese residents in Geneva.*

This, of course, follows the age-old precedent of committing suicide on a man's doorstep because one disapproves of him.

* * *

You're telling us!

A local newspaper's poster:—

JAPANESE
BOMBERS
ACTIVE.

That's what there's been so much complaint about.

* * *

The Will to Wed

BRAVING
WAR TO WED
Colombo, Ceylon.

" War or no war, we are determined to go on to China to marry our boys."

These were the words, to me to-day of the two English brides-to-be held up here on their way to wed, in Shanghai, by orders from the Baptist headquarters in London.

Miss C. Lloyd, of Blaina (Mon), and Miss M. E. Belcham, of Upper Twickenham, were in the middle of a Chinese lesson at the Colombo Baptist centre.

The two girls' bridegrooms-elect, the Rev. J. C. Newton and the Rev. Vincent Jaspar, are working with the Baptist Mission in China.

" The two brides-to-be will have to stay in Ceylon until it is either possible for them to go on or we decide to bring them back," an official of the Baptist Missionary Society in London said yesterday.—" Daily Herald," September 9.

As we have been continually emphasizing, business *must* be carried on as usual.

* * *

The Very Latest

There's a journalist in town who actually has some money in the bank. Yesterday morning, deciding he could make use of some of it, he drew himself out a cheque, and toddled off to the bank to cash it.

He waited, reading a monthly magazine, until he got absolutely fed up, and approaching the paying teller's counter said :—" Here, what about my cheque?"

" Oh, this one?" enquired the teller. " Do you know you have post-dated it?"

* * *

Economy

Then there's the story of the member of the staff of a local firm who became stranded in an outport.

He wired to the head office " Am held up here. Shall be delayed a week."

The firm cabled back " Start your holidays as from yesterday."

* * *

Well, Well, Well!

The following appeared recently under the heading of situations wanted :—

Young Russian lady seeks position as housekeeper in small family, preferably bachelor.

What we want to know is do bachelors usually have small families?

BREAKING THE ICE

"SAPAJOU" & "IN PARENTHESIS" OBSERVE THE WAR

The Real Remedy

A heading in a local contemporary:

KERRAN, BRITISH LABOUR LEADER, DECLARES NO COUNTRY CAN SIT BACK IN " SPLENDID ISOLATION " DURING RADIO TALK

That may be so, but one can always turn the radio off, can't one?

* * *

" Apple and Eve "

Dear I. P. when I've been in doubt,
You've always said, " There is a way out
Of troubles and scraps, of every kind;
Nor should we let them, prey on our mind."
Now if you can solve this riddle for me,
You'll certainly have my affection I.P.
It happened this way (it always does),
The Boy Friend decided to give me a " buzz;"
Said he'd prepared a treat most divine,
A " Russian Light Op'ra," but first we would dine.
Soft music! dim lights! a " gimlet,"—exciting!
A table well set it looked most inviting.
Now the problem which needs to be solved is this,
Please tell me truly, don't you think it amiss
To serve anyone vodka, with a hot Irish stew?
(Perchance Little Audrey gives it to you)
Honestly now, I'm not very capricious,
But I failed to find that stew delicious:
For haven't we all for seven weeks long,
Been in a " stew " with Izzy's loud song?
And shouldn't Vodka be served with black caviar,
Anchovies, stuffed olives, ham—Kolbasar?
The climax appeared when it came to the " sweet,"
When I beheld it I just had ' cold feet '
After vodka and stew, I had to sit there and " grapple "
With a plain rice pudding and a big baked apple!
I think you should tell him it just " isn't done,"
To serve such a mixture and spoil all the fun.
That vodka, stew, rice and apples combined,
Is bad for,
            The Girl He Left Behind.

Shouldn't be at all surprised if the poor dear had a pain under her pinny.—I.P.

* * *

Sporting Note

Apropos of the " Daily Mail's " historic remark in a leaderette on grouse shooting one Twelfth of August—" and the crack of the rifle was heard upon the moor "..... Judging by the incessant popping of the shot-gun upon the Shanghai marshes, the snipe appear to be coming in well.

Boycotter Writes :—

" To me the position is simply this —if the international agreements providing appropriate measures for dealing with an aggressor are still valid, let those measures be applied—and damn the consequences."

With all humility *In Parenthesis* would suggest that it is no good going round damning consequences until you are perfectly sure you can damn them successfully.

* * *

Too Much Interference

We are very much exercised over the protests which are being made to China over the decision to blow up the mole at Chefoo. There may be no military significance whatever in such a proceeding, but after all, what we want to know is *whose mole is it* ?

* * *

Dithyrhambics

" The patron of the ..... is captivated by the general excellence of food served, of the delightful concert music provided during dinner and of the gay lilting melodies for dancing which follow. Subdued lighting carries out intimacy."

Too much of that sort of thing and you don't get carried out! you're thrown out.

* * *

A Policeman's Lot

Our evening contemporary prints an excellent story about the two press photographers, armed with curfew passes, who took a couple of girls out for the evening, and left the restaurant which they attended too late, and were picked up by the police. It is suggested that the photographers got a bit tough with the police, and the story continues :—

" You can go, but the girls will stay here until dawn," was the only result getting tough got the photographers. They finally left for home, minus two girls. They don't expect to call them up again soon. Newsmen when questioned about this defeat at the hands of the police will of course point out the fact that they were *only* photographers.

It looks to us that so far as the two young ladies are concerned the name of press photographers in future will be mud. At any rate, as perfect gentlemen, they should have kept the girls company during their vigil, unless the police threw them out on their ears.

"SAPAJOU" & "IN PARENTHESIS" OBSERVE THE WAR

OVERTURE UP-TO-DATE

"SAPAJOU" & "IN PARENTHESIS" OBSERVE THE WAR

Corroboration

In its report to the Assembly, the Sub-Committee of Thirteen, of the League of Nations, dealing with this Sino-Japanese fracas, says:—

> "After an examination of the facts laid before it the Committee is bound to take the view that the military operations of Japan against China by land, sea and air are out of all proportion to the incident which occasioned the conflict, that such action cannot possibly facilitate or promote the friendly co-operation between the two nations.

It is really astonishing how everybody perceives what the Japanese cannot see.

* * *

Correspondence

IN PARENTHESIS
"NORTH-CHINA DAILY NEWS

Dear I.P.:—You didn't publish my last effort—was it too fruity? Are these any good? I have to do something in my office these days!

> There is a young Welch Fusilier
> Who has a great liking for beer
> He got terribly tight
> When he went out last night
> So to-day he feels horribly queer
>
> There is a young man in the Loyals
> Who's badly afflicted with boils
> When he tries to sit down
> He exclaims with a frown
> Shanghai's sure got me in its toils.
>
> An Ulster who landed in China
> Said "I've never seen anything finer
> Than the Cabarets here
> With cold——Beer,
> And an American girl called Dinah."

I think the last one ought to produce for me a free case of——Beer?

SUFFERER.

Do you really think it will now?— I.P.

* * *

Here She Is Again

Little Audrey blew in the other day following one of Izzy's hates over in Pootung.

"And where have you been now?" we asked anticipating she had been doing something she didn't ought.

"I've been on the flagship, dearie," she replied, brushing her hair back in a nonchalant manner.

"Whatever for?"

"Just looking things over, don't you know? As a matter of fact I was on board when they bombarded Pootung."

"Really! That wasn't a good show. They didn't seem to be registering at all well?"

"Neither would you if you had been in the jam they were in."

"Jam? However do you mean?"

"The fire control officer had mislaid his abacus. Laugh?—I should have died."

* * *

Quick Returns

Sufferer's letter in IN PARENTHESIS on Saturday in which he indulged in a little verse on the subject of cabarets, girls and beer. He mentioned the name of the particular brand. We cut it out, because, we've never got anything out of this column at any time except an occasional dirty look. That morning we received the following complaint from him:—

> What a low trick to have left out the name of the beer in my lovely poem which you publish to-day. But I have an idea. You write to—and tell them it is your poem, and if you get a free case of beer you send it over to me. I'll write to—and tell them it's mine, and if I get a free case I keep it. If we both get free cases we might spend an evening together, and if we don't we won't. A sort of "Wei Wah" bargain, what?

An hour afterwards the brewery which he had mentioned wrote in stating that there was a case of beer available for SUFFERER, if he would get in touch with them. U.B. will please note that their letter has been sent on to him. In the meantime we are wondering if we can think up a good story about a pair of grey flannel pants, because we don't drink beer.—Or, maybe, we can wangle a gold watch.

* * *

The Gentle Answers

The editor of a local contemporary supporting certain crimson hued political doctrines, commenting on the present crisis, concludes:—

> We may see the attitude of Messrs. Araki, Sugiyama, Okada and others. They did not expect any resistance on the part of the Chinese people. Now they have to face the facts, which are contrary to the expectations. And despite the probability of the catastrophic outcome of the war for their country they

"SAPAJOU" & "IN PARENTHESIS" OBSERVE THE WAR

Major-General A. P. D. TELFER SMOLLETT, D.S.O., M.C.
Commander of the British Forces in Shanghai Area

decided to put everything at stake: either to win or to commit harakiri on the fields of Great China. We hope the second way will be their fate.

Pleasant sort of bloke, ain't 'e?

* * *

These War Reports

The only effective way to obtain the truth about what is happening around Shanghai is to read the newspapers published in the interior, if and when they reach here. The following was published in a Hankow journal:—

> Shanghai, Sept. 25. (Central)—The Chinese forces are indisputably gaining the upper hand in the war in Shanghai. The Japanese troops, after having been repeately defeated at Lotien and Liuhang, are in very low spirits and have for the fourth time asked for reinforcements. The new troops, numbering about 40,000, have practically all arrived, and it was announced by the enemy that their fourth general offensive would be started on the 25th instant. However, the fighting at the front to-day is by no means more fierce than it was during the last few days.
>
> In view of the fact that they have already defeated the Japanese forces several times, the Chinese troops are quite sure of winning the victory. The Japanese reinforcements this time mostly come from Formosa and Korea and their fighting ability is no better than that of those who came before them. If they dare to attack the Chinese lines, they are bound to be defeated again.

That's the stuff to give the troops. Relinquishing lines of defence is apparently the best way of proving how completely the enemy is licked. Obviously retreats are advances,—backwards.

* * *

Regrets

An N.Y.K. shipping notice:—

> Consignees and cargo owners are hereby notified that the mv. "Kagu Maru" discharged her cargo for and via Shanghai into registered lighters at this port at buoys Nos. 14 and 15, for eventual storage at the N.Y.K. Wayside Wharf. Due to tense situation then prevailing, however, the cargo working at the wharf was rendered impossible. Subsequently the bombardment in the district has compelled the crew of the lighters which moored near the wharf to free ashore and later it was discovered that the lighters with cargo aboard were all missing.
>
> All the efforts we since made to locate the lighters have been fruitless, to our regret.

They really mean much to the regret of the consignees and cargo owners. They will, of course, realize that cargo and lighters mizzled off while in their custody.

* * *

Business as Usual

The following notice has been sent to a renter of land on Point Island, by the Whangpoo Conservancy Board:—

> Shanghai, Sept. 29, 1937
>
> Dear Sir,
>
> *Re Temporary Lease of Land at Point Island*
>
> I beg to inform you that the temporary lease of land to you at the Point Island, Canal side, Lot No.—($3\frac{3}{4}$ mow for gardening purposes and $\frac{1}{4}$ mow for erecting hut) will expire on the 30th of September, 1937.
>
> If you wish to renew the lease, please remit to the Board the following amount which is to be paid in advance.
>
> $—for one year's rental of $3\frac{3}{4}$ mow for gardening purposes.
>
> $—for one year's rental of $\frac{1}{4}$ mow for erecting temporary hut.
>
> Total $—for one year's rental of 4 mow.
>
> Unless you renew the lease on or before the 15th of October, 1937, the land must be vacated and the fence and hut removed.
>
> Yours faithfully,
>
> CHIEF ENGINEER.

That is, of course, if the fence and hut have not already been violently shifted.

* * *

A Correction

> "Big shells, whizzing across the river, exploded with terrific detonations which rocked buildings on the Bund" writes a contemporary describing the bombardment on Thursday evening.

The staff of this journal having experienced all the bombardments during this present spot of trouble are quite unanimous in stating that the buildings don't rock,—they merely quiver.

"SAPAJOU" & "IN PARENTHESIS" OBSERVE THE WAR

REAR-ADMIRAL REGINALD VESEY HOLT, D.S.O., M.V.O.
Rear-Admiral, Yangtze

"SAPAJOU" & "IN PARENTHESIS" OBSERVE THE WAR

These Victories

> The truth, according to the spokesman, is that the Japanese invaders have suffered repeated reverses in the hands of the Chinese, and at the end of their wits are fabricating false reports nobody except themselves would believe.

There's quite an art in fabricating an untruth which you can believe yourself.

* * *

Care Wanted

> "The Art of Law and Other Essays Juridical and Literary," is the title of a book recently published locally.

If law is thus going to be allowed to count as an art instead of a science, it is possible that ballet dancers and other such wild fowl will be heard protesting.

* * *

Hurrah!

> Tokyo, October 10.—A letter of encouragement and gratitude to the Japanese newspapermen who are covering the hostilities in China will soon be dispatched by the Society for the China Problem, Domei learns on good authority.

Nobody ever thinks of encouraging other foreign newspaper correspondents. Just fancy how much better we should all feel if only someone would pat our backs and stroke our fevered brows!

* * *

Correspondence

IN PARENTHESIS

"NORTH-CHINA DAILY NEWS"

Dear I.P.—Thanks so much for sending me the credit note for U.B. Beer. I would have asked you to share it with me on my Embankment Building verandah in the next air raid, but as you prefer other things to beer, this might be of assistance.

I.P.'s lost the seat of his pants
And the springs of his watch are worn out
  In giving Shanghai
  A laugh and a cry
So what about helping him out?

If the pants are too long, send them over to me; and if you get two watches, I'd like the gold one!

SUFFERER.

Shanghai, Oct. 11.

Begins to look as though it's becoming a bit of a racket, doesn't it?—I.P.

* * *

These Martial Courtesies

From a Chinese daily report:—

> Torrential rain has failed to dampen the spirit of the opposing forces in several isolated points along the southern bank of Wentsaopang.

Now, if the Japanese would only find something nice to say, what a beautiful war this would be?

* * *

Very Many Thanks

In a review of the recently issued "Shanghai's Schemozzle" the "Shanghai Evening Post & Mercury," in the course of a series of very agreeable remarks, says:—

> "After reading through the whole and looking at the cartoons, many will agree that the way Sapajou and In Parenthesis 'observe the war' is the sanest way after all."

Well, after all! And what we mean to say is this, many years ago Elbert Hubbard published in his very excellent magazine "The Philistine" the following very wise remark:—

> "Don't take this world too seriously; you won't get out of it alive, anyhow."

* * *

A Small Request

IN PARENTHESIS has one very small request to make of the opposing commands. Amongst other things he keeps some budgerigars, and as a result of recent casualties, two are left in a somewhat large cage, a lady budgerigar and a gentleman budgerigar. They appear to have been talking things over, for yesterday she got busy effecting a few improvements in her nesting box.

Would it be possible, do the opposing commands think, to take "time off" for a few weeks, so that whatever she is contemplating can be brought to perfection? A little more quietness is necessary!

BALLISTIC OR ATMOSPHERIC?

"SAPAJOU" & "IN PARENTHESIS" OBSERVE THE WAR

The Tale of Cock and Bull

The "Sydney Sun" which perpetrated the wonderful picture of Shanghai's burning Bund following Black Saturday, is responsible for the following, which appeared early in September:—

> Charging into the Japanese guns at Shanghai, the Chinese overwhelmed 60,000 Japanese.
>
> They broke their lines at five places and forced their way to the banks of the Whangpoo River, where they threaten to drive the Japanese across the river.
>
> According to the latest advices from Shanghai it is asserted that the Japanese have been pushed back along a front of 15 miles on a total front of 25 miles.

We shrewdly suspect that both the Chinese and Japanese spokesmen have been keeping something hidden from us.

* * *

A Clean Sweep

The evacuation of foodstuffs from Hongkew is being carried out so thoroughly that only the other day we saw a lorry loaded with pig iron. That's a nourishing thought, isn't it?

* * *

Of Course

> "Japan's activities in China, being of a self-defensive nature, do not form a violation of the Kellogg and the Nine Power Pacts high officials of the Foreign Ministry indicated to-day."—telegram from Tokyo.

It is not generally known that this self-defensive action by Japan was dictated by fear that China was preparing to invade that country.

* * *

Comic Relief

That proclamation by the Japanese Commander-in-Chief convinces In PARENTHESIS that something in is the wind. He concludes:—

> With the close co-operation of the naval forces, the Japanese Expeditionary Force is determined to clear the skies of ominous clouds and I am confident that the day is not so far off when the light of peace will shine again.

Wasn't it Maurice Chevalier who used to sing something about "Standing on top of a rainbow, sweeping the clouds away?"

Looking Ahead

Mr N. M. Hubbard, president of the U.S. Navy League has been "talkin' wiv his mouf," according to a United Press telegram:—

> He painted a lurid picture of Japanese plans of expansion, saying that the Japanese after conquering China would attempt to take the Philippines, Sumatra, the Malayan Peninsula and Hawaii and finally the United States.

Mr. Hubbard has apparently overlooked the island of Yap.

* * *

The Prodigals

> "Neutral observers estimated that the display staged by the Nipponese warships used up at least U.S. $3,000 worth of ammunition."

Just chucking money about, that's what they're doing.

* * *

Tuesday's Bombing

From a contemporary:—

> In other words the Japanese pilots were running no chances of diving into a direct line of heavy 50-calibre machine-gun fire.

Of course they weren't, and why should they?

* * *

The Changeling

Reports the United Press:—

> The Committee for the maintenance of order issued a proclamation here (Peiping), yesterday, changing the name of Peiping back to Peking, signifying the northern capital.

Sort of "Off again, and on again, my name's Flanigan."

* * *

Horticultural Note

From a local advertisement:—

> Warehouse receipt No.—issued by Kailan Warehouse for 50 tons special Kailan coal seed.

It is devoutly hoped that the receipt will be found so that the coal seed will be available for the spring planting.

MAJOR NAOKATA UTSUNOMIYA
The Japanese Military Spokesman in Shanghai

"SAPAJOU" & "IN PARENTHESIS" OBSERVE THE WAR

Real Comfort

From " Finance and Commerce" in an article dealing with the local situation :—

> " While, therefore, no one can deny that Shanghai is in for hard times if the war is prolonged, such hard times do not mean collapse or anything like it."

Such a statement as this is definitely unfair to our Jeremiahs, who are hard enough put to it to spread their lamentations, without this sort of discouragement.

* * *

Household Hint

A letter to the editor :—

> I shall be grateful to anyone who could give me a good recipe to destroy cockroaches, or at least keep them away.

Well, so far as we can see it all depends what you really want to do. The cockroaches we wish to destroy we shoot, those we wish to keep away we give a nasty look. Probably the most effective way of killing the little devils is with bathbrick. The method is quite simple. You first catch your cockroach, turn him over on his back and holding him thus, firmly, read this column to him. When he laughs pop a small dose of powdered bathbrick into his mouth, death being instantaneous, if not quicker.

* * *

This Mysterious Schemozzle

From " Great Britian and the East."—

> Interesting reports are heard of Chinese aeroplanes flying over and dropping bombs in Japan. The writer has reason to believe that four of them did thus visit Nagasaki, though without doing much damage. There is no reason why they should not. From Shanghai to Nagasaki is 465 miles. Close by are the important coal mines, ironworks, and shipyards of Moji. Say 1,000 miles for the round trip—not at all an excessive distance—and luscious rewards to be gained in giving the Japanese a taste of their own medicine.

We do think the Chinese spokesman should have told us all about it, instead of keeping so quiet.

* * *

The Female of the Species

Tamie-san, a patriotic waitress of the Cafe Shinko, on Kotobukicho, Tientsin, has been giving her impressions of the warfare in that district, Referring to the aerial bombing of that city, she is reported to have said :—

> " It was a most thrilling sight. From the roof top of the Peiyang Fantien on Kotobuki Road, I watched a unit of Japanese warplanes conduct an aerial bombardment upon the Chinese positions in the city including the Municipal Government Building, the Tientsin Central Station, the Nankai University, the Telephone Office, and others. That was on the morning of July 29.
>
> " ' Every shot tells' was the word for the Japanese bombardment. It was just like seeing a moving picture. How I enjoyed it ; it was really the experience of a life time."

It is a pleasant thought that someone enjoyed the bombing, isn't it, Tamie-san ? Bloodthirsty little beauty !

* * *

The Artless Abbot

Chao Kung, Trebitsch Lincoln to you, has organized a League of Truth which, of course, is a very proper thing for an abbot to do, and in connection therewith he has issued circulars, up to the present two in number. In the second Chao Kung writes as follows :—

As a buddhist Abbot I declare :

> Even if all the propaganda fabricated and disseminated against the Japanese were true (and they are not true), those who conquered India, Burmah, Ceylon, etc., etc., etc., those who hold in subjection Nations and Races all over the world ; those who have, in turn, violently and unjustly interfered with the life and destiny of Portugal, Spain, Holland, Denmark, France, Germany, Italy, Russia, Persia, Afghanistan, Tibet, China,—Ireland, etc., etc., etc. ; those who deliberately broke their pledged word solemnly given to the Jews,—those have no right to play the rôle of holy indignation against a chivalrous, well-intentioned and spiritually superior race like the Japanese.

From the significant omission in this passage it is clear that his love for Great Britain is just as inveterate as ever.

* * *

An Enquirer Writes

We all know that the battle of Waterloo was won on the playing fields of Eton

SHANGHAI'S "MOONLIGHT SONATA"

but is the battle of Shanghai going to be won on the golf course at Hungjao.

We really don't see why it shouldn't, if it wants to.

* * *

Bliss

"Seeing that heavy casualties had been inflicted on the Japanese, the reports stated, the Chinese troops contentedly dropped back to their original positions."

"Something attempted, something done, had earned a night's repose."

* * *

A Funny Business

And then there was the man who one evening listened to two broadcasts on the subject of the pleasant little game they are having around Shanghai, and came to the conclusion that there was not one, but two wars in progress.

* * *

The Aesthetes

Shanghai, Oct. 5 (Reuter)—A spectacular Chinese air-raid brought to a climax to-day's heavy fighting... The tracer bullets and exploding shells provided a beautiful pyrotechnic display for watchers in the foreign areas.

There is just a chance that the artistic side of this pleasant little bickering stands in danger of being over-emphasized.

* * *

'Ow 'Orrible

From Mr. A. de C. Sowerby's letter in a recent issue:—

At the moment, however, it would appear that Shanghai business men and merchants have been stunned by the catastrophe that has befallen them into a state of inertia and are supinely awaiting the final stages of that catastrophe. Perhaps it would be fairer to say that they are trying to carry on and patiently hoping that something may turn up to save them from their impending doom.

Lawd luvaduck, Arthur! You aren't 'arf makin' our flesh creep.

* * *

These War Correspondents

It was only a short while ago that we got to learn of the stories which some correspondents were sending abroad about the local contretemps. Some of them have "done themselves proud" in the matter of highly exaggerated descriptive writing. Another proof of this has come to hand in a letter from abroad:—

"I don't know where you can be sleeping, as, according to the newspapers, there's not one brick on top of another in Shanghai."

Of course the writer did not realize that in its wonderful cellars where the bombing and shelling have not interfered with one brick being below another, Shanghai has ample accommodation.

* * *

Circulation

It is not often that I adventure into the realms of Heavy Industry (writes Dr. Archibald Grubb, LITT. D.), but the development of the scrap iron industry is interesting.

Australia has for some time been selling her scrap iron to Japan.

Japan is now unloading it on China.

China may yet profit by collecting it, selling it to Russia, and thus creating a new avenue for Chinese trade.

Russia may then unload stocks on Japan.

Thus modern civilization develops a theory of the Circulation of Scrap Iron to show how far we have progressed since Harvey discovered the circulation of the blood!—Peter Persnurkus in the Sydney "Sun."

* * *

Great Concern

The "Shanghai United News," the only Japanese newspaper here now, is much interested in the manner in which the Chinese Liberty Bonds are being sold. It then goes on to comment on the cost to China of carrying on hostilities as follows:—

Referring to the expenses being sustained by the Chinese Government in carrying on hostilities, the paper asserted that the daily cost is approximately $3,500,000 for the Shanghai area only. The monthly expenses, the journal adds, will exceed $100,000,000. "How," the paper asked "can the Nanking Government continue paying out such huge war expenses?"

If the newspaper's estimate is correct, then China appears to be spending £6,000,000 a month around Shanghai. It is reported that Japan's expenses for the whole of her military adventure totals £1,000,000 a day, so that sup-

ANOTHER RUBICON CROSSING?

"SAPAJOU" & "IN PARENTHESIS" OBSERVE THE WAR

posing China were spending at the same rate, her northern defense campaign should cost her about £24,000,000 a month. But Nanking knows a thing or two better than that.

* * *

That Caption Again

RISING HEAVYWEIGHT FALLS ON POINTS.

A most painful proceeding!

* * *

What Do they Mean?

Mr. Ikeda (who is being added to the Japanese "brain trust") is considered to be one of Japan's foremost financiers and most successful harmonizers.—United Press.

One of these days we'll give him a party and he can assist us in singing "Sweet Adeline."

* * *

Correspondence

IN PARENTHESIS

"NORTH-CHINA DAILY NEWS"

Dear I.P.

INSECTS ARE NOW USED AS ORNAMENTS

Does the above apply to all insects, or are husbands not fashionable as yet?

Yours to a turn
A WORM

Shanghai, Oct. 14.

* * *

IN PARENTHESIS

NORTH-CHINA DAILY NEWS

Dear I.P.

Yesterday when I was musing, Little Audrey (of "Izzy" fame) appeared suddenly before me.

"My! My!" she said in her quaint way, "what are you doing there, big boy? Have you seen this?"

She showed me a placard with these words:—

"MAJOR OFFENSIVE LAUNCHED BY JAPANESE."

"Well," she asked me, "what do you think of it?"

"Hm-mm," I replied, "I pity the poor Major for the ducking he received. I fear he will catch a cold."

Little Audrey chuckled merrily and glided with swan-like grace out of the room.

Yours musingly,
GENTLEMAN FRANK.

Shanghai, Oct. 13.

* * *

Somebody Happy

A gentleman writing from Denver, U.S.A. to a local contemporary:—

You certainly are having a terrible time there in Shanghai just now. But it may interest you to know that the resistance to the Japanese which the Chinese are putting up very much delights everyone here with whom I come in contact.

The thought that the local what's-its-name is giving delight to people so far away, is just the one thing which makes everything seem so much brighter.

* * *

And Quite Right Too

A protest against the imposition of high war risk insurance rates on cargo consigned or shipped for Japan has been sent by the Japanese Marine Insurance Underwriters to the similar organization in London. Japanese insurance bodies object to the inclusion of Japan, as well as China, in the war zone.

Some sceptics still don't seem to believe the Japanese statement, so often reiterated, that this is not a war. The London insurance underwriters seem to be bent on taking advantage of Japan's kindness,—to China.

* * *

Naivete

There's quite a lot of ingenuous propaganda being pumped out by both sides to this imbroglio, but the following from Nanking fairly takes the biscuit:—

"Emperor Hirohito was said to have not concealed his anxiety over the recent unfavourable developments of Japan's foreign relations during audiences granted to Mr. Hirota and General Sugiyama, Foreign Minister and War Minister respectively.

And those two gentlemen, knowing the necessity of keeping such a matter a deep secret, immediately went out and "blew the gaff." We don't think!

"SAPAJOU" & "IN PARENTHESIS" OBSERVE THE WAR

A THOROUGH GOOD ROASTING

"SAPAJOU" & "IN PARENTHESIS" OBSERVE THE WAR

Colney Hatch

We are much enamoured of the story of the three American scientists, who are reported to have discovered an anæsthetic shell as a means of stopping war. The report goes on:

> After one of the adversaries had intensely bombarded the opponent with these missiles, the front line could go over to the enemy camp with trucks, pick up the sleeping warriors, and make them prisoners.
>
> After this method of warfare had been used successfully by both opponents, and when each side had captured all their adversaries, the war was bound to come to an end owing to lack of combatants.

Reads like a piece of damphoolishness to us.

* * *

Dear Old Cal Again

"After achieving their objective, the Chinese soldiers *did not choose* to stay in their newly occupied area, but retired to their original positions."

* * *

More Blood Curdling

> "The foreign controlled Shanghai of to-day stands within a ring of opposing military forces, and all the wishing in the world will not alter the fact that those of us within that ring are exposed to stray bullets, and anti-aircraft shells and, perhaps, to wind deflected or badly aimed bombs from aeroplanes."—*From a contemporary.*

It's a horrid thought, but cheer up, dearie, you can always dodge those things when you see them coming.

* * *

Why Not?

Just another delightful caption:—

MEDICAL GROUP
WILL DELOUSE
REFUGEES HERE

And while they're about it they might delouse this "Impending Doom."

* * *

A Wise Precaution

A contemporary goes on record as stating that the Japanese are drawing on newly-made munitions.

And quite right too, no sensible commander would dream of using up all his matured-in-the-wood stuff straight away.

Now you tell one

> Replying to a question posed by one of the correspondents whether the continued bombing of Chinese positions in Chapei had any effect, the spokesman answered that the principal effect has been a great demoralization of the Chinese forces.

So much is this the case, In Parenthesis is able to confirm, that the Chinese forces have been so thoroughly frightened that they are quite unable to leave Chapei.

* * *

And Talking of Delousing

What about this actually issued by Domei, the Japanese news agency? . . . . . .

> Tokyo, Oct. 15.—(Domei) Four leading figures in Japan's public lice left here to-day for the United States and Europe. .

With the descent of hundreds of thousands of Japanese into China can it be said now that the latter is suffering from Phthiriasis? That's what we call a lousy question.

* * *

What Ho!

The "China Press" had the following in one of its editorials:—

> "The only Japanese newspaper in Shanghai, "The Shanghai United News," has taken the liberty to belittle the progress which has been witnessed in the Chinese public subscription to the Liberty Bonds. What this war-time upstart in the journalistic world thinks of this patriotic loan is of no interest to us; it is more than welcome to entertain any illusion either for self-gratification of for self-deception."

So now the wretched little squirt knows exactly where it gets off.

* * *

We Like this one

We read in the Municipal Gazette the other day:—

> Owners of factories who have moved machinery and plant into the Western District of the International Settlement are invited to communicate with the Industrial Section of the Shanghai Municipal Council for advice and suggestions.

"SAPAJOU" & "IN PARENTHESIS" OBSERVE THE WAR

THE NOVICE

How nize! We can fancy an owner of plant and machinery writing in as follows:—

"I am troubled with housemaid's knee. What can I do about it?"

They will then look up Form No. 13a "Knee, Housemaid's" reading simply:—"Sack the housemaid."

* * *

Correspondence

IN PARENTHESIS

NORTH-CHINA DAILY NEWS

Sir,—With reference to ANTI-COCKROACH's plea for a recipe for the extermination of those awful pests, I would like to offer a few suggestions. These methods are a bit brutal but very effective, I can assure you.

If the cockroaches are of the "tough and can take-it" type, then he will have to resort to the chloroform and hammer method. On the other hand, if they are of the ordinary weak household variety, just a little powder will suffice.

Of course, some cockroaches get into a house with the idea of establishing a colony, and this is the type where there is no hope or remedy. The Japanese in Hongkew, however, have, so they tell me, found a solution. They with the aid of a little kerosene and a three copper box of matches just burn the whole house down. Very effective. This is all right in a way, but most people want to keep their house.

In conclusion, I hope ANTI-COCKROACH will appreciate my suggestions.

ANTI ANTI-COCKROACH.

Shanghai, Oct. 13.

* * *

How Very Charming!

"Chinese troops on the north bank of the creek were engaging another detachment of enemy forces......"

This is called, in the military textbooks engaging tactics.

* * *

Mobilization en masse

Nanking, Oct. 15.—(Central)—After a brief respite on October 13, rivers in Hopei resumed their spectacular rise yesterday.

Merely showing, after all, that Japanese actions in north China have even irritated the rivers. We have only to wait until the mountains walk, and then there will be trouble.

The Real Dignity

From a leading article in a local newspaper:—

"The increasingly apparent likelihood that Japan's military "muckamucks" have bitten off a much larger portion of the China 'pie' than they can chew is being demonstrated daily on both the Shanghai and North China fronts."

Well, after all, no one expected a china pie to be anything but indigestible.

* * *

We are strongly

In favour of the proposal to hold a mass meeting in Shanghai in connection with the spree that is at present proceeding. Shanghai ought to make it very clear to the world that it thoroughly disapproves of what is going on. There may still be some people who think we are enjoying it.

* * *

The Delights of War

From the Hankow "Herald":—

The fighting at Pingyuan in Shansi is reported to be very fierce yesterday and serious losses have been inflicted upon the enemy forces. Chinese reinforcements have arrived at the front and are looking forward to exterminating the enemy there in a short time.

Happy anticipation, no doubt!

* * *

Social Note

From a correspondent:—

Seeing that so many of the evacuees have returned to town, I think that you should enlighten them as to what has been what in the "social world," during their absence. So,—

The Whangpoo threw a party and boats by hundreds came,
The flagship, cruiser, submarine and craft by every name,
Missiles soon spread carange: things didn't go as planned
Miss Shrapnel led the dancing: Miss Idzumo led the band.

* * *

Something Wrong Somewhere

HOLY SEE CANNOT TAKE SIDES

Tokyo, Oct. 15.—He had not received instructions from the Vatican that Catholic missions should assist in Japan's fight against

CALL IT "NO MAN'S LAND"?

Bolshevism, Mgr. Paul Marella, Apostolic Delegate to Japan, said to-day.

He added that the Holy See did not take sides in any political controversies throughout the world.

Nevertheless, he declared, Japan's "fundamental opposition against Bolshevism was in unison with Catholic ideals, and a Japanese victory over Bolshevism would first benefit China and, eventually, the whole world."—Reuter.

Considering Japan is not fighting Bolshevism but China, the reverend monseigneur seems to be talking through his very clerical biretta.

* * *

A Remonstrance

Jack Cade wrote the following letter to the Editor who passed it over to us :—

I was *MOST* disappointed when your tame humourist missed such an opportunity for one of his irresistible jokes occasioned by little Oswald's presentation of Irish confetti at Liverpool recently. And wouldn't one about a close season in British officials for Japanese airmen have evoked a response ?

Couldn't he have had fun over the superior marksmanship of the Liverpudlians and pulled the legs of the bold machine-gunners on having failed to bag a lady passenger !

Unless the lad looks to his laurels I'll have to patronize "Comic Cuts" again.

Oh, come orf it, Jack. We declared a close season for Ambassadors last month and we had something to say about the bricks heaved at the Oswald. We can't, unfortunately, declare a close time for other officials, because they do not appear to be protected by the British game laws.

* * *

Correspondence

IN PARENTHESIS

NORTH-CHINA DAILY NEWS

Dear I.P.

"Several high police and British officers visited the scene in the afternoon."

This is not the first time a term associated with fish or meat in a certain state has been used in your august journal. The feet of the police have at timesc ome in for adverse comment, but here the correct term surely is big, not high. Then the British officers—surely not high, perhaps tall, but never, never high, even if block houses are bathless. These dangerous times, with so much sickness about, one can't be too careful, and before tipping off the Health Department could you reassure me that all is quite quite healthy with our gallant guardians ?

TORPEDO.

Shanghai, Oct. 15.

* * *

How very true !

So much, writes a correspondent, has been written about the frightfulness of Japan ; well it all seems desperate at times, but on the footing that "all is fair in love and war" it seems clearly definite that all nations throughout the world in time of future wars will be henceforth compelled to do, at some time or other, the very same deeds which are being enacted by the Japanese military forces around Shanghai in this undeclared war.

This present diversion being in the nature of a demonstration of sincerest affection, everything goes !

* * *

The Blinding Flash

". . . . let me say there is always two sides to a question just as there are two sides to a quarrel which actually means it takes two parties to make the necessary quarrel either for a street fight or a national fight as the case may actually be found to be correct."

Like all generalities the above is not entirely true. Take shadow boxing, for instance !

* * *

Zeus Nods

The Hongkong "Daily Press" has dropped another brick. Just read this :—

Stories not altogether devoid of thrills, although far away from the scene of war, were brought to Hongkong yesterday by wives of naval officers who returned here from their annual summer vacation at Wei-hai-wei, the former German colony, which is now a British possession.

With his hand on his heart, In Parenthesis wishes to assure the editor of the paper in question that it wasn't, and it ain't !

NANTAO'S GOOD SAMARITAN

"SAPAJOU" & "IN PARENTHESIS" OBSERVE THE WAR

Wei-hai-wei to Hongkong

According to Mrs. O'Flynn, wife of Surgeon-Captain J. A. O'Flynn, of H.M.S. Cumberland, in an interview given in Hongkong

> "there are over 100 foreigners, including many women, absolutely 'bottled-up' in Wei-hai-wei."

All we can say is "Thank goodness for that little word 'up.'"

* * *

'Quitter'

> *Dear I.P. How would you,*
> *Like to be taken to the zoo*
> *On your birthday, for a treat,*
> *And have a big cream cake to eat?*
> *This is the tale I want to tell,*
> *Now you know the Boy Friend well.*
> *He said to me, "Sure as fate*
> *My pet, I'll keep this precious date."*
> *Saturday he wasn't busy,*
> *Promised inspection of the 'Izzy,'*
> *After we would 'do' a show,*
> *There's little else left now you know.*
> *However I was satisfied*
> *To have my wishes gratified.*
> *After lunch I must confess*
> *I spent an hour on my dress:*
> *When, tinkle, tinkle, went the bell,*
> *And I wondered, what the—*
> *Can it be he's sent a chit,*
> *And want's to wriggle out of it?*
> *I read the letter out to 'Gran,'*
> *"Sorry, sweetheart, to spoil the plan,*
> *Circumstances unforeseen,*
> *Hinder me my little queen."*
> *'Granny' watching anxiously*
> *Suggests the zoo, cream cake and tea;*
> *On my birthday, like a kid*
> *That was just the thing I did:*
> *Even ate too much cream cake,*
> *It's given me 'uncomfy' ache.*
> *'Gran' of course is such a sport,*
> *But don't you think, the Boy Friend ought*
> *To make an effort once a year*
> *To be with me? I sadly fear,*
> *'Little Audrey,' would be bitter,*
> *If once you proved to be a 'quitter':*
> *Please tell Boy Friend, to bear in mind,*
> *The 'date' with*
> > *The Girl He Left Behind.*

* * *

To-day's Great Thought,

From to-day's leading article:—

> "With one accord merchants who identified themselves with Shanghai repudiated acceptance of any such policy of scuttle."

In other words coal may scuttle, but the Shanghai merchant never!

* * *

More Comforting

> Cakes, candies and cigarettes, as well as good cheer, were given to the "boys" at the front by Misses Toyoko Hayashi and Kishino of the Shanghai Girls' High School, who in company with Mr. Jumpei Hashimoto and an instructor of the school, made a round of the front lines.—News report.

As the two young ladies left, they were astonished to hear the troops burst into:—

> Mesdemoiselles from Yangtszepoo
> How are you?
> Mesdemoiselles from Yangtszepoo
> How are you?
> Mesdemoiselles from Yangtzsepoo,
> Now you know a thing or two.
> Mesdemoiselles from Yangtszepoo!

(Parenthetically it may be mentioned that this is the result of a change in the brand of our birdseed).

* * *

Inevitable Conclusion

We don't believe there is a word of truth in the allegations that both sides are using poison gas. All that we have noticed has been an unusually large amount of hot air liberated.

* * *

This Ghastly Business!

> "36 HOURS TO KILL"
> OPENS AT SHANGHAI

Keep your seats, ladies and gentlemen! It's quite all right. The above is merely the heading to a cinema review in a Hankow newspaper.

* * *

A Foolish Question

"Who's the laziest man in the world?" asks a correspondent, who really ought to know better, and then goes on to supply his own answer:—"The taipan who got his clerk to work out his cross-word for him."

Of course, it's all wrong, because there was the taipan who wouldn't even take that much trouble.

COMPARING NOTES

"SAPAJOU" & "IN PARENTHESIS" OBSERVE THE WAR

The Old Gag

"Japanese forces in the Hongkew and Yangtszepoo areas are there to defend those sections of the International Settlement assigned to them under the Joint Defence Scheme and are not "occupying" the Settlement zones north of Soochow Creek, Japanese naval and diplomatic spokesmen emphasized at a press conference Monday morning."

Well, we suppose, after all they must have their little joke.

* * *

Worser and Worser

"The lull was believed by military circles, however, to be an ominous calm presaging another impending storm."

You know this local "it-hurts-me-more-than-it-does-you" is getting more and more serious. Last week we were treated to an impending doom, and now they are handing us out an impending storm.

* * *

A Little Psychology

From a speaker in Hongkong:—

Generally we can say that everything that has made you think, that has made you astonished, that you find unbelievable, that you find offensive or that has made you laugh to death, you won't forget for your whole life.

That's why we shall always remember the little bit of fun some people are having round Shanghai!

* * *

Natural History

"Since Shanghai newsmen could not very well cover the local 'incident' at the war fronts in person, seeing that their sight appeared to cause military authorities great revulsion, press conferences came into being," reports a local contemporary.

The military authorities have In Parenthesis's deepest sympathy. He has always maintained that newsmen at any time are a shocking sight.

* * *

More Frightfulness

From a contemporary:—

CHENGTU, Oct. 8.—On Sunday, the entire city of Chengtu was benagged. It seemed that a Chinese hag was hanging from almost every house, shop, school, or public building in the city. The occasion was the departure of over 100,000 Chinese soldiers from Szechuen. They are to proceed to east China and join in the war against Japan. During the day a special farewell was held in one of the public parks of Chengtu.

It may be all right to benag a city, but isn't it a bit hard to hang the hags?

* * *

This War of Words

A Japanese spokesman is quoted as saying:—

In answering allegations that the Japanese airforce has taken part in indiscriminate bombing, it should be pointed out that whereas the Nipponese have always carried out their raids during daytime, the Chinese make their flights at night. When night raids are conducted, visibility is naturally very poor, and it would appear that under the circumstances, and not even taking into consideration the poor marksmanship of the Chinese, inaccurate bombings are bound to take place.

It seems to us, though, of course, we may be entirely wrong, that the less anybody says about the marksmanship shown hereabouts the better.

* * *

A Very Mad Madrigal

When this "incident" is over,
Oh, how happy we shall be,
And we shall no longer dither
When we take our morning tea.
Business will again be brighter,
Once more we'll be on the spree,
And the Chinese will be making
Friends out of the enemy.

When "impending doom" has passed us,
And we start to count the cost
Of this nasty little rumpus,
We shall know just what we've lost.
We shall miss the evening's air-raids,
Miss old Izzy on the bust,
And enjoy the sparkling sunshine
Free from bombing, smoke and dust.

When we've finished this schemozzle
We can get back to our jobs,
And at night-time quietly sozzle
While we think of those queer "yobs,"
Posing every day as spokesmen
Inspiring newsmen with surprise,
At the funny tales they tell them,
Which they bluntly scepticize.

"SAPAJOU" & "IN PARENTHESIS" OBSERVE THE WAR

ANOTHER DANGEROUS SECTOR

"SAPAJOU" & "IN PARENTHESIS" OBSERVE THE WAR

Not So Happy

"However, as reported yesterday, the Japanese consider it 'merely a matter of time before the Chinese retreat.'"

That's what we have been thinking, but it seems to be merely a very long time.

* * *

The Gipsy's Warning

A local heading :—

Dr. Young Says Ostrich-Like 'Isolationists' Who Bury Heads In Sand Will One Day Have Their Feathers Burned

Yes, but it won't be their head feathers, will it?

* * *

That Bromide Again

Concerning the bombing of the railway administration building :—

"The building has been badly damaged but is still standing."

"Bloody but unbowed" eh? There you are, we got it in first this time.

* * *

Happy News

"Chinese military observers here viewed the Japanese move (on Tazang) as strategically sound, but materially, the adventure will prove to be very costly."

The Japanese will undoubtedly be glad to learn that, from a purely technical point of view, they are quite correct.

* * *

Comic Turn

"The spokesman (Japanese in Tokyo) waxed caustic concerning Japanese press reports that Japan was considering denouncing the Nine-Power Pact. Japan, he emphasized, was still observing the terms of the pact (under which the signatories undertook to respect the sovereignty, independence and the territorial and administrative integrity of China).

The dear chap is trying to make us laugh again. As we have a split lip, we do wish he wouldn't.

* * *

When the Ink Flies

This slight unpleasantness which is occupying everyone's attention at present has spread to the correspondence columns of the local press, with "Tiger" Kanai getting in some heavy stuff. Listen to this :—

"It has been Japan's purpose never to aggravate situations but to promote a better understanding, and to prevail on China to end her provocative acts and challenging attitude."

And we, too, know somebody in whose mouth butter won't melt.

* * *

Journalistic Endeavour

"Time," the very pert American weekly news magazine, is becoming altogether much too imaginative, judging from a map of Shanghai which it published in its issue of September 30. According to its cartographer the U.S. Consulate is still in Hongkew, though apparently it does not know it. The U.S.S. Augusta is moored off the Japanese Consulate, instead of the Idzumo, Broadway Mansions is situated at the junction of Hongkew Creek and the Whangpoo, and north of it at that, the Custom House and the Shanghai Club have changed places, and the American Club is situated on Nanking Road, but on the south side of that thoroughfare, so it's not only us that Izzie has been making dizzy in this present what-you-may-call-it. But when they produce a photograph of Gen. Wu Teh-chen, and a lady and label it "Mayor O. K. Yui and wife," it just proves that things are getting too terrible for words.

* * *

Correspondence

In Parenthesis

"North-China Daily News"

Dear I.P.—

The following may be of interest for your column.

It was discovered just last night by a few of our friends who were doing a little abacus work and this is what they finally achieved :

(1) The Mukden Incident started September 18 and the Chinese have always referred it as   9 1 8
(2) The Hongkew war January 28, 1932, referred as   1 2 8
(3) The Lukuchiao Incident on July 8, referred as   7 8
(4) The Shanghai (present war) Hungjao Incident, as   8 1 3

                        1 9 3 7

"SAPAJOU" & "IN PARENTHESIS" OBSERVE THE WAR

KISMET

"SAPAJOU" & "IN PARENTHESIS" OBSERVE THE WAR

You will no doubt perceive that the above figures represent the month and dates of all the incidents, and adding the whole sum giving a total of 1937, and which, according to the Chinese, this is the year when the Japanese are being made to pay. In other words the day of reckoning has come.

Lt. M. B.

Shanghai, Oct. 19

We think it's crazy, too!

* * *

Reassurance

In case there should be any anxiety as to who really has control of the air hereabouts, In Parenthesis, wishes to assure both of his readers that either side is in full command.

* * *

Difficult Travelling

Writes a correspondent in Chucheng:—

> Last week two 'planes, presumably Japanese, passed and repassed at a very great altitude, travelling from north to south and vice versa.

All of which just goes to show how versatile these aviators are getting nowadays.

* * *

And Then Again

"Time" perpetrates the following:—

> "Because the International Settlement has its own wires direct to the world, it is the first major engagement of modern times to be reported without censorship."

Oh yeah! Only a little over a month ago the absence of censorship led to 62 words being excised from one message.

* * *

Something We Want to Know

The representative of a local American brokerage firm commenting on the New York Stock Exchange collapse, has delivered himself of the following:—

> The market isn't functioning as a market any more, as there is no buying—only selling."

Now, what we want to know is how can there be no buying if people are selling?

The Liars!

From a Japanese paper:

> According to a Hongkong telegram to the "Asahi," it has been revealed that three nationals of a certain Power were aboard a Chinese plane which was shot down by a Japanese plane during the air raid on Canton on Wednesday. Two of them were killed outright, while the other is lying in a critical condition. The Canton authorities, the message says, who are greatly embarrassed by the revelation, are trying to mislead the world by giving out false information to the effect that the machine in question was a Japanese one.

The taradiddling in this "incident" is getting more complicated.

* * *

Hostile English

Chinese is easy to learn if you have a system. So is English: all you have to do is to classify your events under a few standard phrases. Thus:

> *Fierce fighting.*—Any attack where a lot of noise is made.
> *Driven off.*—Any retreat.
> *Details are not received.*—Any situation whereon you have no dope.
> *The building was gutted.*—Any fire even if the structure had none of those things and wasn't burned out anyway.
> *Withering fire.*—Any machine-gun performance.
> *Terrific hail.*—Any flight of bullets.
> *Tension.*—Anything that starts rumour-mongers going.
> *According to information reaching here.*—Any rumour.

* * *

Tripe!

The Hongkong "Daily Press," which every day seems to work itself into a frantically high temperature, recently got the following off its chest:—

> With all their boasting the Japanese have reduced their lavishly publicised first-class nation to the level of a third-rater. All the leather-lunged pronouncements by Konoye, Hirota and Party have proved shallow as a drained dam. The outpourings by Hirota particularly can conveniently be classified in that branch of deceitfulness known as clumsy

"SAPAJOU" & "IN PARENTHESIS" OBSERVE THE WAR

DEPRESSING DAYS

"SAPAJOU" & "IN PARENTHESIS" OBSERVE THE WAR

lying, and that is indeed remarkable in the case of such an adept so carefully trained in a country where lying is one of the fine arts—if not actually regarded as one of the finest!

As a valuable contribution to the sober discussion of China's present troubles, this might do very well boiled with onions.

* * *

Correspondence
IN PARENTHESIS
"NORTH-CHINA DAILY NEWS"

"Dear I.P.—Can you solve a problem which for some time has worried me (although it has not caused me sleepless nights)? What is the meaning of the phrase I frequently see used in the local press, "Shanghai's younger set"? I know what is meant by the phrase "A drunken set"; I have heard the phrase "A set of china" — small C. please Mr. Printer—but the phrase "Shanghai's younger set" has me beaten. How is it manufactured, and when you have got it how is it used? In general terms how would you classify it?

Yours inquiringly
PUZZLED.

Shanghai, Oct. 21.

Shanghai's younger set, Puzzled, consists of our local "chickens."—I.P.

* * *

IN PARENTHESIS
"NORTH-CHINA DAILY NEWS"

Dear I.P.—Your exposure of the journalistic endeavours of "Time" regarding our schezzschrem—damn it all—schemozzle is deficient in only one respect. The picture isn't the Idzumo either.

F.A.P.

Shanghai, Oct. 22
Some journalism, eh?

* * *

Essential Qualification
Judging from developments in the local propaganda war, it would seem that the most important quality which an official should possess is that he should be a good denier.

Remarked a Club Man
Gazing reflectively across the Whangpoo and referring to the destruction wrought in Pootung :—

"We are certainly living in stirring times."

Several of our friends are in the consomme, too!

* * *

Too Terrible for Words
A correspondent writes pointing out that at the At Home on H.M.S. Danae the guests were thrilled witnesses of an air-raid by Chinese at which the Japanese batteries fired with their anti-aircraft guns.

Apparently the guests were in danger of being "shot away" in more senses than one.

* * *

The Warring Spokesmen
"Chinese reports of advances made by General Han Fu-chu on North China fronts are fabrications, as the Shantung general is now in actuality busy digging in on the banks of the Yellow River. Other reports of Chinese advances in the vicinity of Shanghai are also false, and all Chinese counter attacks were repulsed by the Japanese yesterday with the attackers suffering heavy losses."—*Japanese report.*

Now it is again China's turn to " tell one."

* * *

Blimey!
"A Chinese military spokesman announced that Chinese forces on both sides of the Japanese salient at Kechiapailou and Kuangkang south of the creek were closing in behind the Japanese line."

Quite early in the war we pointed out that this was quite likely to happen, and should the Chinese successfully close in behind the Japanese line, the newer military method of facing the enemy back to back will have been perfected.

* * *

On Geography
Village names in the pleasant little bickering around Shanghai are more than a little difficult to keep track of. Especially is this the case with the village the Japanese are so eager to capture and the Chinese so determined to resist :—

DAHZANG
TAZHANG

DISCONCERTED CONJURER

"SAPAJOU" & "IN PARENTHESIS" OBSERVE THE WAR

TACHANG
DAZANG
TAZANG
CHAZANG

After all, why not call it Tarzan and have done with it?

* * *

Of Course Not

"That wasn't a bomb which fell in Sinza Road on Saturday" remarked little Audrey yesterday morning at breakfast.

"What makes you say that?" we asked.

"Here I have it on the very best of authority. Doesn't the newspaper say that the Japanese spokesman stated that it was not a bomb, but merely a small petrol tank?"

"But do you always believe what official spokesmen tell you?" we asked scornfully.

"Always," was the terse reply.

"Very well, and why do you?"

"What's the use of having official spokesmen telling you anything if you don't believe it?"

"Well, I think that story about the petrol tank's a bit thin, you know."

"Yeah," remarked little Audrey, "most tanks are, when you come to think of it."

"I mean the story. They say it was a small emergency tank holding only a few gallons. Whatever could they want it for? That's what I want to know.

"Ah! There you are. You don't seem to remember that aviators find petrol very useful for keeping the old school tie clean, do you?"

And little Audrey gurgled in her coffee cup.

* * *

Correspondence

IN PARENTHESIS

"NORTH-CHINA DAILY NEWS"

Dear I.P.—Many thanks for your description of the oft-used phrase "Shanghai's younger set." If the younger set is composed of Shanghai's chickens, am I right in concluding that the "smart set" (often referred to in social news) is composed of the hens and their opposite sex who often adorn our social functions?

A SEARCHER AFTER TRUTH.

Like any other fowl we dislike being drawn!—I.P.

* * *

These War Editorials

From the Tokyo "Nichi Nichi":—

"Whether or not we shall capture Nanking of course depends on the decision of the army authorities, but the complete sweeping away of all the Chinese forces on the Shanghai front is conclusively believed to be a hard blow at the anti-Japanese regime in Nanking."

They're telling us!

* * *

Quarantine Measures

We are glad the Council has issued that notification about foot and mouth disease. We had noticed something of the same sort of trouble in the bar before the dinner hour, but on reflection have come to the conclusion that it isn't foot and mouth, but hand and mouth disease which is prevalent there. You know—"All the same for everybody, boy." Chronic sufferers may be quickly spotted by their oft repeated cry of "Wattle?"—being, of course, the terser form of "Wattleyouave?"

* * *

A Correction

From a Central News Agency dispatch:—

"Earlier reports that Japanese bombs meant for the wharf (Pukow) all dived into the Yangtze is partially incorrect, because while some of them did drop into the river, others hit the wharf."

This correction is still incorrect. In Parenthesis has it on the best possible authority that bombs don't dive.

* * *

We Will Now Carol

"Earlier in the evening, Chinese batteries in Chapei opened up on the Japanese lines heralding the offensive."

Listen to the Chinese cannon,
  Heralding a new attack.
Hear machine-guns gaily singing
  Their refrain of smack, smack, smack.
Now they're starting in Chapei
  Fighting at the close of day
Listen to the cannon's roar
  As they've never roared before!

This harmonious overture
  Prelude to another fighter fight
Making Chapei not so happy
  Through the long autumnal night,—
Heralding is what they're doing
  Unlike angels are they singing
Devilish voices of the night
  Giving us another fright!

"SAPAJOU" & "IN PARENTHESIS" OBSERVE THE WAR

DEPRESSED INDUSTRIES

"SAPAJOU" & "IN PARENTHESIS" OBSERVE THE WAR

The Blind Eye

The Foreign Office spokesman in Tokyo, commenting on the Hongkong enquiry into the sinking of fishing boats by the Japanese Navy is reported to have said :—

> "Self styled Chinese fishermen of the junks attacked have testified that the junks were equipped with one to four old-style cannon.
>
> "We have never heard of a fishing boat with such armaments. The Chinese testimony, therefore, must be taken as a confession that the allegedly attacked junks were pirate junks which infest the neighbourhood of Bias Bay."

That the spokesman has not heard of fishing junks plying out of Hongkong carrying small cannon to defend themselves against the China coast pirates is deeply to be regretted, but the argument he seeks to develop from his lack of knowledge is, just the same, one of those fruity old birds known as a *non sequitur*.

* * *

Correspondence

IN PARENTHESIS

"NORTH-CHINA DAILY NEWS"

Dear I.P.—Even though bearing in mind the exhortation by H.M. Prime Minister, Mr. Neville Chamberlain, "not to allow our minds to be deflected by hypothetical things that have not arisen," which he declared in winding up the House of Commons debate the other day on Far Eastern events, I am nonetheless assailed with a gnawing doubt concerning the tail end of Reuter's summary published by your collaborators. Reuter's report quotes Mr. Anthony Eden, H.M. Foreign Secretary, as closing with these words :

> "To talk now about what will be included and excluded from the Brussels Conference in advance will be most unwise. We have a definite agenda given us by the League, and the proper procedure to follow is, in consultation with other signatories of the Treaty, who will all be present, *to do the utmost lying in our power to discharge its mandate.*"

The italics in the last lines are mine. I might add that Mr. Eden's ultimate and perhaps most cryptic remark of all, as Reuter reports it, is that, "If the conference fails, then we shall enter into a new situation, which we shall have to contemplate."

What I want to know and seek from your experts on F.O. business, is if this is all evidence of a new tendency in Christendom or a fresh approach to Buddhism, Nirvana and all that? Or not? If so, what? Also, why?

ALOYSIUS M. HIMMELBACHSTEIN JR.

P.S. Could you also ask Little Audrey about all this?

A. M. H. (jr.)

Dear Aloysius, what very peculiar questions you ask! The passage you italicize is to be read "to do the utmost recumbent in our power," etc. The word "lying" in this instance, has no reference whatever to propagandist prevarication.—I.P.

* * *

Very Terse!

> "The sound of explosions was so deafening that the dropping of individual bombs could no longer be distinguished."

Well, who wanted to, anyhow?

* * *

Our City Fathers

From a statement issued by the S.M.C. :—

> "Any suggestion of shortage is, therefore, entirely misleading and probably made for profiteering purposes."

Come on lightning! We told you that ten weeks ago!

* * *

Somewhat Unkind

> "In yesterday's operations Japanese bombers ignored their pledge not to fly over the International Settlement south of the Soochow Creek."

This continual "picking" on the Japanese must really stop. As In Parenthesis has already pointed out, if the International Settlement will not sincerely co-operate with the Japanese authorities and keep the settlement from under the Japanese planes, complaints of this nature are bound to continue.

* * *

In an Article Headed

CATHAY THEATRE
BALCONY USED
TO STORE TEA

the following passage occurs :—

> "Owing to the construction of the picture palace which has all seats on the

"SAPAJOU" & "IN PARENTHESIS" OBSERVE THE WAR

WORLD CHAMPIONSHIP

ground floor and no balcony accommodation."

That's what we like about this modern journalism. You pay your money and take your choice of what you believe.

* * *

The Brighter Minds

Some of the output of the world's thinkers has to be seen to be believed. One Frederick Whyte is reported to have said :—

> If the war continued much longer and Japan came to the market for oil, Great Britain and America could tell her that they offered her no public humiliation through the operation of economic sanctions, but if she refused to meet them at the conference table they would apply an oil sanction against her.

It is only the highest type of genius which can find public humiliation in a number of sanctions, and something essentially private in the application of one.

* * *

This Love Pidgin

"Quite a little love drammer in the classified ads. this morning." remarked Little Audrey while filling her face at breakfast yesterday.

"What do you mean, now?" we asked, looking up from our piece of the paper.

"Why this P and Claude business."

"Hm! I don't see much drama about it. Only a couple of young people at 'outs' over something."

"Oh! But it's much worse than that. A romance has definitely been broken."

"Very well, then, I suppose you've got some fantastic idea in you're head. Out with it."

"Don't be so impatient Ip. It works like this. You see P.—which might mean Peggy, or Phyllis or even Polynesia,—had a date with her young man, Claude. Her papa has ideas of his own. Either he disapproves of Claude, or he wanted P to stay home and darn his socks, or something. Anyhow she didn't get out to keep the appointment. Obviously the girl loves Claude, for no young woman in her seven senses would waste money apologizing, if she didn't. So what does she do? Why, she hirples along to your office and sticks in a classified ad. Here it is :

> 'Claude, sorry detained yesterday, father difficult, please arrange another day. P.'

Nothing could be nicer."

"Yes, that's all right, but what about the broken romance?"

"Well, you see. Claude turned up at the appointed spot, and hung round in the rain. No P if you please. Hangs around for about an hour or so, fed up to the back teeth, and at last he drifts round to your place and ticks her off in the personal column :—

> 'Philanderer. The answer is "rats" !'

"All I can say if that doesn't put P off her oats, the girl has no dignity whatsoever. So you see romance busted."

"But Audrey, supposing you broke an engagement like that, wouldn't you apologize?"

"Me? Apologize to any of my twirps? I've got 'em trained, big boy. Why, if I am an hour late for an appointment with any one of them, he immediately apologizes for being too early.

"Gawd, I wouldn't like to be your husband."

"'Nobody axed you, sir, she said' Anyhow I wish I knew that chap Claude. I'd massage the back of his head with a brick."

And, chuckling gently, Little Audrey was soon immersed in the cross-word puzzle.

* * *

"Inside the Tiger"

"Do not suppose that because Japan goes on raining havoc upon the helpless wherever her Furies can reach, she isn't simultaneously trying to persuade those bad Chinese to give in and get under.

"For instance, this is good, from the former Japanese Minister in Sweden, Mr. Shiratori :—

> "To speak of a greater ideal. I would like to suggest that China abolish all the armaments throughout the country and entrust Japan with the maintenance of peace and order. . . It is my belief that, if left in charge of Japan, China will certainly find herself more strongly defended than otherwise."

"It is *our* belief that, if you were left in charge of a hungry tiger you might find yourself quite warm and comfortable—*inside* the gentle creature."—"Daily Mirror."

* * *

The Apostle of Love

Abbot Chao Kung—Treb. the Linc. to you—has founded the League of Truth, which he says is "for TRUTH, JUSTICE, KINDNESS" and "against LIES, INJUSTICE, HATRED" and when he is not singing a soothing sutra to himself, or murmuring a mournful mantra, he

"SAPAJOU" & "IN PARENTHESIS" OBSERVE THE WAR

BACK TO NORMALITY

writes beautiful pamphlets. No. 3 is just off the press, and is another example of the truth, kindness and justice which the Treb. has discovered after a meteoric career through various creeds. The following is part of his most recent lucubration :—

> "My dear Generalissimo, you are once more the victim of deceitful slogans, dinned into your ears by interested foreign nations. 'War is Hell,' — said an American General. Don't you a military man know this ? War is Hell and it is only hypocritical Great Britain and their lie factories (their newspapers) who pretend that war can be 'humanized.' I am against all wars, precisely because it is hell for humanity. But Great Britain is not against war and wars, they glory in it. Even now while they denounce alleged Japanese 'atrocities,' they are preparing similar or greater atrocities for the next war."

Now, now, now, Treb! You may have all sorts of grievances against the British, but do you think you are doing any good by massacring the English grammar ?

* * *

Downcast

This war is gradually getting us down. We actually got out of bed the other morning to have a look at an air-raid !

* * *

We Like This Little Bit

> "Literally the sky was black with Japanese planes which rained bombs in unison. It was estimated that the total number of Japanese planes thus taking part could not have been less than 100, the spokesman said."

We've noticed, ourself, that the sky is very black when 100 aeroplanes are up.

* * *

Asses on Horses

It is to be noted that, despite warnings, and the tragic affair in Keswick Road on Sunday, horse-riders have again been seen in the district. They may think they are very brave and all that, but as regards brains they seem to have the mentality of the common or garden louse !

Our Fans

As we remarked a while ago we have quite a fan following. Some write in to us and just recently we have been securing telephone fans. The first was a woman. We guessed that from a voice, one of those nice deep contralto voices, that sort of voice we could stand crooning a lullaby to us in our more emotional moments. We shall hear it again one of these days. Well, anyhow she had a story for us which duly appeared, and if she thinks of any others will she please ring us up; we'd like to hear that voice again.

Then on Sunday we were sitting with our spade and pail in the drawing room listening to the children's hour of the radio,—we always do that on Sunday, sort of getting back to nature for a while,—when the telephone rang and a man's voice asked us if we were In Parenthesis. We replied, quite coyly, that we were, and he remarked he had a stunt for us. Couldn't we have a letter written to us asking if it were true that the Japanese had changed the name of Woosung Road to Hunki Dori ? Well, after all, and so to speak, what we mean for to say is, well there it is, but what it means we don't quite know. Anyhow here's another part of this column filled in for the day and that's somep'n.

* * *

Black Faced Interlude

Old man Whangpoo,
Dat ole man Whangpoo,
He mus' do somep'n,
But can't do nuth'n,
But keep on rollin', jus' keep on rollin' along.

You an me, we sit and strain,
Listenin' to bombs come droppin' again.
One bursts here, another bursts there,
An' shrapnel falls jus' everywhere.
We are weary and sick of fightin'
An' watchin' planes go gaily flightin'
While ole man Whangpoo,
He keeps on rollin' along.

There ain't no tradin'.
Wiv bills of ladin'
We can't do nuthin',
But must do somep'n
To keep on carryin', yes, keep on carryin' on.

You an' me, we're all at sea
Some of us already in the consommee.
A sad face here, another one there,
Unhappiness permeates the air.

"SAPAJOU" & "IN PARENTHESIS" OBSERVE THE WAR

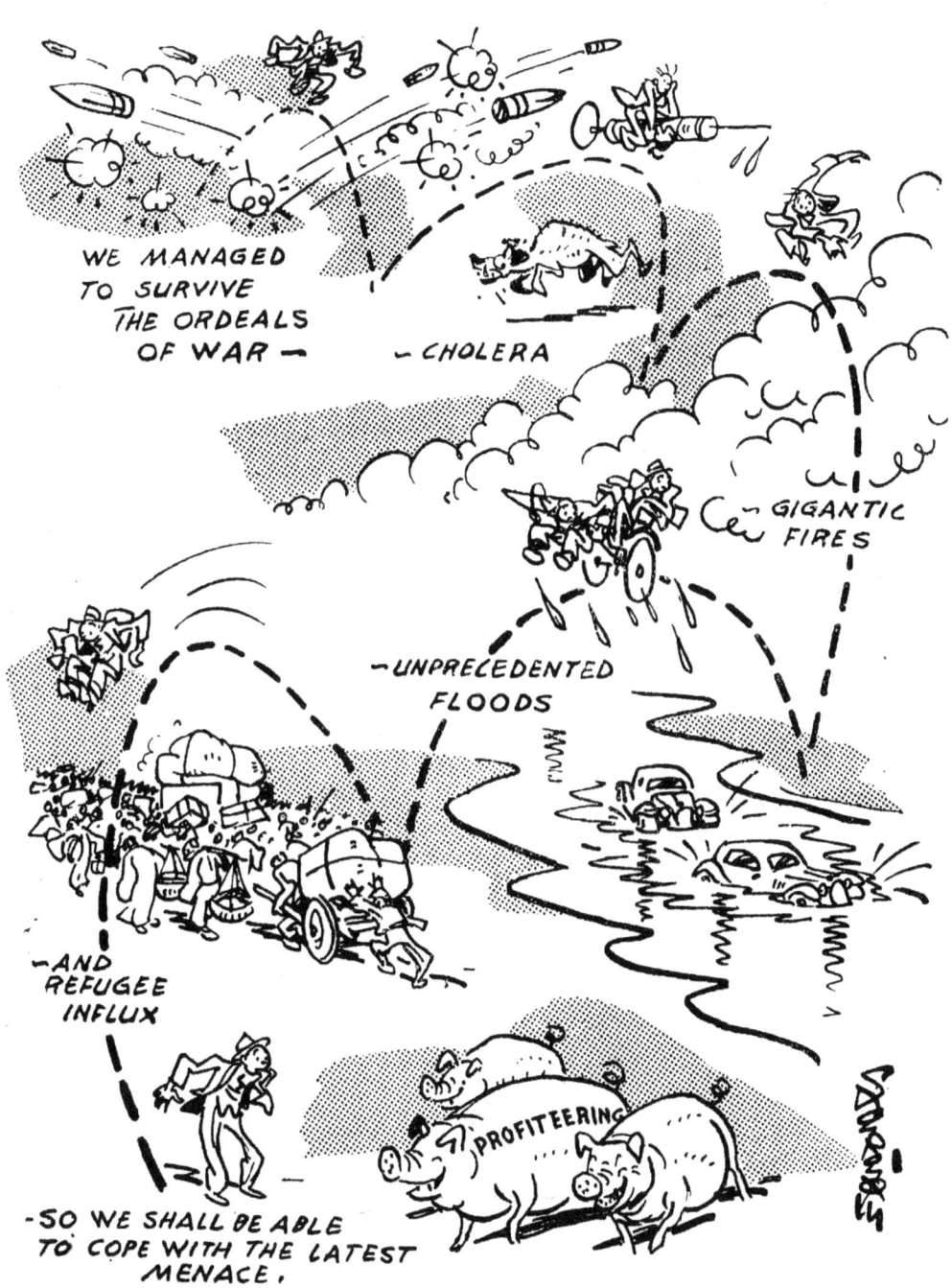

SHANGHAI RESILIENCE

"SAPAJOU" & "IN PARENTHESIS" OBSERVE THE WAR

If only Izzie, would jus' get busy,
An' cease from makin' our heads so dizzy,
Then we, like Whangpoo,
Could go on carryin' on.

* * *

The Fountain of Youth

A local caption:—

AUTONOMOUS REGIME FORMING; LEAGUE TO GET "LIBERAL AUTONOMY"; JAPANESE FOSTERING SCHEME TO "REJUVENATE" MONGOLIANS

I.P.:—Boy, page Dr. Voronoff!

* * *

It was a very bright move

On the part of the Chinese command to mislead the enemy on Tuesday night by appearing to be moving troops up to Chapei while in fact they were moving them out, but is it quite nice to deceive people in such a way?

* * *

A Little Praise

For the writer in a local contemporary who managed to describe the Chapei conflagration without dragging in the well-known bromide "blazing inferno." Everyone missed the more forceful "flaming hell," but, then, there are still people who believe such an expression is hardly polite.

* * *

Let's Gloom Awhile

Now the war has wandered
Far away from here,
We in quietness settle
To our evening beer.

Night now falls so gently,
Darkness shrouds the sky,
No more fires are blazing,
Planes don't fly up high.

There hasn't been an air-raid
Since the last full moon,
By the rules of warfare
We should have one soon.

Whangpoo still looks gloomy
Curfew's yet imposed
Half a hour to midnight
Cabarets are closed.

So now all good children
Early go to bed;
Fighting's done a mizzle
"Peace" is here instead.

Journalistic writers
Spilling lots of ink,
Settling all our problems.
Succeeding? We don't think!

* * *

A Warning

I.P. wishes it to go on record that the Chinese are co-operating with the Japanese. The latter wanted them to leave Chapei and now they have done so.

Any more official statements to the effect that Japan wants more sincere co-operation from the Chinese, and we shall be so annoyed that we shall have to take a bite out of the mantelpiece.

* * *

Mere "Gup"

In an editorial on the campaigns in China a New York magazine "China To-day" has the following:—

> The Chinese Red Army has developed the manufacture of innumerable small bombs and grenades too small to kill. They are placed in abandoned houses as the enemy advances, to explode when invading troops sit on chairs or open cupboards, with most disturbing effect.

If there is any truth in this statement, the practice should be immediately stopped. This is certainly no time for practical jokes of that sort!

* * *

A Wallop All Round

A local contemporary

> Notes the perturbation and regret of the Japanese authorities over the Keswick Road incident;
> is gratified over the anxiety shown by appointing a Court of Enquiry;
> critical of the British Military and S.M.C. for not issuing warnings, and
> critical of the Consular Body for not telling everyone what it is doing.

It appears to have overlooked the soldier through whose cigarettes a bullet passed. He should be reproved for smoking!

* * *

Correspondence

IN PARENTHESIS
"NORTH-CHINA DAILY NEWS"

Dear I.P.,—Do you have any objections if I take a pot shot at some of these Japanese aeroplanes with an anti-aircraft

"SAPAJOU" & "IN PARENTHESIS" OBSERVE THE WAR

THE NEW ORCHESTRA

gun? In case you have no objections, can you tell me where I can borrow one? There ought to be a few somewhere around the International Settlement that are not in use.

You see, I.P., I want to test a theory of mine, namely, that I can do as well with one of these contraptions as certain parties, whom I will not mention by name, over in Hongkew. I am even conceited enough to think that I might do better if a book of instructions—something on the order of a Ford Manual—were included as a part of the equipment of the anti-aircrafter and also provided you will let Little Audrey help me a bit. Clever child that.

Now please don't let me down, I.P., or I will never read your column again. You see I take my theories seriously.

TIRED PHILOSOPHER

Shanghai, Oct. 26.

Really, old man, this continual criticism of the anti-aircraft shooting around Shanghai must stop. It is so terribly unjust, for one thing, for to the best of our information both sides succeed in hitting Shanghai every time. And we don't know where you can borrow an Archie, though we can lend you a catapult if you want it.—I.P.

* * *

A Daniel Come to Judgment!

"In matters of attire Eve has a habit of getting her own way," writes a local editor.

And only in matters of attire, Mr. Editor?

* * *

Writing on the Question

Of restarting Hai Alai a correspondent says:—

"In my opinion it certainly would not be cricket for foreigners to foist the game on the public during such times as these."

Naturally it wouldn't. The game, so far as we understand the matter, is hai-alai.

* * *

These Pigs Came to Market

Much fun, it is reported, was had when a small herd of pigs got through the barbed wire of the French Concession, and bolted in all directions, through the streets; so with due apologies to Charles Kingsley, we'll carol a bit.

A swineherd came rushing up to the barbed wire,
Up to the barbed wire as the sun went down,
With sows and a boar and eight little pigs
To find them a refuge within the great town.
For pigs have lives, and so have men,
And when the troops go they'll be fattened again,
With empty abattoirs moaning.

A soldier stepped out from his sandbagged post,
From his sandbagged post as the pigs came up,
And said " Wot-the-ell are you tryin' to do?
I cannot let you and them damned pigs through.
For orders is orders, and we 'ave bin told
You can't come through 'ere for love nor for gold."
The swineherd started groaning

But somehow or other the trick was worked
The trick was worked and the pigs got through
And all of the herd were soon on the run,
Bystanders were laughing to see the fun.
For orders is orders, but pigs is pigs,
And now all those porkers are in their new digs
Little Audrey's merrily la-ahfing.

* * *

Good Gracious!

Heading in a Hongkong newspaper:—
 ATROCITY PILED
 UPON ATRACITY

Gawd! ain't it terrible what this call-it-anything-you-like is doing to some proofreaders!

* * *

The Better 'Ole

Reads a local heading:—
 BRITISH NOT TO
 BOLSTER POSTS
 ON PERIMETER

Of course not: sandbags are *so* much better.

* * *

For the Life of Us

We cannot see why Japan's refusal to accept the invitation to attend the Nine Power Conference should be described as curt. After all it consisted of 800 words and was accompanied by a 2,000 word statement explaining why they declined.

To have been thoroughly curt they should merely have replied " No."

"SAPAJOU" & "IN PARENTHESIS" OBSERVE THE WAR

THE KEYS OF THE CAPITAL

"SAPAJOU" & "IN PARENTHESIS" OBSERVE THE WAR

Self-Answering Question

"Can you pollute thought with Government propaganda and expect a citizen to tell the whole truth?" asked Mr. Herbert Hoover in a recent speech.

Yes, Herb. you can. And you may punish a citizen for not telling the truth whether he's polluted or not.

* * *

The Dear Old Abbot

We can't resist just one more reference to the latest outburst of Chao Kung—Treb. the Linc. to you—in Circular No. 3 of the League of Truth. Here is another of the higher periods from the monkish pen:—

> But what do some of the occidental nations care about such things? What is the welfare of the Chinese People to them? They are only interested in dividends, in money making, that is all. *The Japanese, on the other hand, are interested in your welfare;* they know you, they understand you, they sympathize with you, *they really and truly want to help you.* How do I know this? Can I read their thoughts, their secret thoughts? Yes, I can read their secret thoughts, *by the openness of their actions. I see what they do here, and by their actions I judge them. And I see that they have come here to help the Chinese People.*

That, boys and girls, is what I.P. has been trying to tell you these long, weary ten weeks. The Japanese have come to help the Chinese people—to all sorts of fancy destruction.

* * *

A Sextette of Quatrains

It was an autumn evening,
  When I.P.'s work was done,
He sat with Little Audrey,
  A'basking in the sun.

O'er Chapei, smoke was rising,
  As it had done all day,
When up spoke Little Audrey—
  "Tell me, I.P., I pray

" Now who has won the victory,
  And what's it all about?"
"The Japanese have won, dear;
  The Chinese are in rout!"

" But what are they all fighting for,
  And why do people hate
Each other as they seem to do,
  And not co-operate?"

" Ah, Audrey, there you're wrong, dear;
  These people are in love.
Affection does dictate, sweet,
  That they should push and shove."

"Is that, I.P., why mamma
  With tiny strap and buckle
Demonstrates her mother love?
  If so, why I should chuckle."

* * *

Explanation

The attitude of the British military with regard to the Japanese desire to send war vessels up the Soochow Creek appears to be "You can't do that there 'ere."

* * *

Dr. C. T. Wang Says

"The Chinese people have made up their minds to fight to the last man and to the last bullet."

On this it might be remarked that the side which has one man and one bullet more than the other will indubitably win.

* * *

These Military Terms

Writes a contemporary:—

"The hectic battle yesterday and last night, although it could not be described as a co-ordinated campaign. . . . ."

We have noticed ourself that it is very difficult to call a hectic battle any such thing.

* * *

General Henry J. Reilly

Is a specialist on Far Eastern Affairs, and expresses the following opinion:—

"One must not be surprised if countries having the means and the will to go to war adopt a forceful attitude, for they are certain of getting what they want without even having recourse to war."

It takes a Far Eastern Specialist to realize that Japan is getting what she wants without going to war.

"SAPAJOU" & "IN PARENTHESIS" OBSERVE THE WAR

THE OLD DRAGON BACK AGAIN.

"SAPAJOU" & "IN PARENTHESIS" OBSERVE THE WAR

A Threnody

Big Ching ! Big Ching !
What a terrible thing,
*   Your clock it won't work,*
And your bells they don't ring.
*   Is it because of this undeclared war,*
Which all of us find such a terrible bore ;
*   Or is it because you don't want to tell*
The time to the enemy fighting like hell ?
*   Big Chung ! Big Ching !*
An astonishing thing
*   To quieten the bells,*
Which surely should ring !

*   Big Ching ! Big Ching !*
Let me tell you one thing,
*   We miss the sound*
Of your chimes ding-dong-ding.
*   Is it because in this soldiers' furore,*
Which most of us say is, after all, war,
*   You've decided, at least for a time, to surcease*
From tolling the hours until Time can bring peace ?
*   Big Ching ! Big Ching !*
Now be a good thing,
*   And tell us the time.*
So Big Ching ! Please ring.

* * *

Assurance

With regard to the shells which struck the "North-China Daily News" building yesterday morning. In Parenthesis, having been authoritatively assured that though the edifice appears to have been in the line of fire, there is no *real* danger to be afraid of, has decided not to evacuate, at any rate for the present. However he would like those responsible for the mishap to understand that he is strongly in favour of it not happening again.

* * *

Of Course Not

A Correspondent, Y, writes in pointing out the difference between the estimates of this journal and a contemporary of the number of aeroplanes which bombed Chenju on October 27, pointing out that there was a difference of fifty between the two figures given. He concludes :—

> "Why be so mean ? Is not 150 just as true as 100 ?

That's what we say. What's fifty aeroplanes between friends, after all ?

Protest

From a letter in Friday's correspondence columns :—

> If Disappointed instead of wasting valuable newspaper space, spent an hour or two a day alongside the members of the Orchestra when they are in a very practical way contributing towards the defence of the Settlement he would have considerably less to say about "Catholic Ecclesiastical Modality," "Whatever" as I.P. would say, "that means ?"

Why he drags us into this musical dispute we cannot for the life of us see, and, anyhow what does it mean ? And what's more, while we're about it, might we mention we don't like this continual carping at Respighi. After all, a man who can write music which no one can understand must be so much cleverer than the ordinary run of music-mongers.

* * *

The Explanation

"It is time, Mr. Spokesman,"
*   The Press-men said,*
"For you to treat us just right,
*   And yet you repeatedly tell us such fibs ;*
Do you think that we're, all of us, tight ?"
*   "Years before," Mr. Spokesman replied,*
" I was a journalist too,
*   And the fibs that they fed to me then*
I'm now passing straight on to you."

" We are young, Mr. Spokesman,"
*   The journalist cried,*
" And the news that we send must be right
*   And yet you've incessantly tried*
To pass us the bunk, day and night."
*   " I've discovered," the spokesman replied,*
" Good stories are never exact.
*   That's why I've continuously tried*
To mix up some fiction with fact."

* * *

Correspondence

IN PARENTHESIS
"NORTH-CHINA DAILY NEWS."
Dear I.P.—
            Municipal Orchestra
              A criticism

Although Respighi has earned a rest, there is still a woeful lack of topicality in programmes.

"SAPAJOU" & "IN PARENTHESIS" OBSERVE THE WAR

"EXCUSE ME, AM I INTRUDING?"

"SAPAJOU" & "IN PARENTHESIS" OBSERVE THE WAR

Now that a crusade is on in poor Cathay, these musical gems immediately suggest themselves:

1. "She wouldn't do what I asked her to, so I socked her on the jaw."
2. "You made me love you—I didn't want to do it.
3. Sullivan's "Gondooliars" (two O's, please, as in McIntyre) will soothe the nerves of the victims of Official Spokesmen.

Yours,
JACEE
(Nom de musique)

Shanghai, Oct. 29.

* * *

Science Note

These captions again:—
FISH'S MIND DISCOVERED TO BE SIMILAR TO MAN'S

Conversely this provides the reason why some men are called poor fishes.

* * *

A New One

A United Press message from Brussels says:—

"The Tokyo Government openly has professed that it does not want to crush China but to "force her co-operation with Japan and by the same token to force her away from Moscow."

From which it appears that China's knees are to be left alone.

* * *

Perfect Arithmetic

".... the Japanese claim that about 100 dead bodies were subsequently found in the buildings. As some 380 men managed to make their way to safety within the defence lines of the British sector, it is believed that the original force concentrated in the godowns was approximately 500 strong."

Audited and found correct!

* * *

How Very Unkind!

Dealing with the text "Should a man full of talk be justified?" a local preacher is reported to have said

"Job was full of talk, but he wasn't saying very much."

To make a remark about a man who talked forty-two chapters worth, to our mind, resembles a very nasty "slam."

* * *

What Ho! She bumps
SOVIET PROTEST
EXPECTED OVER
BORDER CLASH
JAPANESE VERSION CONTRADICTS IN MOST DETAILS
EACH CALLS OTHER THE AGGRESSOR

By calling each other aggressor, they seem, diplomatically to be calling each other something else as well.

* * *

These Proverbs

Changing the subject from the welter-weight championship of the Far East which is being decided hereabouts, shall we consider the question of proverbs for a moment? Most of these glib sayings are not only trite but as statements of fact have to be very closely watched. Thus for example, one that has been bothering us for quite a long time:—

"It's a long lane that has no turning."

Can you think of anything more of a half lie than that? Is'nt it also true that:—

"It's a short lane that has no turning?"

We've seen lanes which weren't long enough to get even half a turning in.

Then again:—

"Birds of a feather flock together."

Of course they do. If you were a flock of birds and only one feather between you, you'd never leave the bird wearing it, for fear it would be missing when it was your turn.

Then again take the remark that:—

"It's a wise child that knows it's own father."

Isn't it equally true that

"It's a wise father that....

(Proof-reader.—Better cut out that last bit. The poor lad's feeling Mondayish)

Well anyhow we could go on with this sort of thing indefinitely, and if any of our readers can invent a few we'll award to the best endeavour one of the nice round holes the shells made in our building on Sunday morning.

LIFTING THE CURFEW

End of the "War"

This little thing was handed in, by an unknown correspondent, for us to handle:—

M.:—Do you know that the local war will end within ten days?

S.Y.S.:—Of course I know. I have heard it for the last three months. I wonder if I.P. knows?

One of the local commanders-in-chief is reported to have stated something to that effect, but he was apparently not taking the Siccawei fathers into account.

* * *

The Health Dept.

We always enjoy reading municipal reports, and that turned out by the Public Health Department is always delightful, following the precedent of Dr. Noel Davis who wrote so charmingly about bowls and pear-shaped gentlemen. In the latest effusion something is said about "frozen suckers." Barnum is alleged to have remarked on the number born every second, but made no reference whatever to their temperature. Or are we all wrong again?

* * *

These Pleasantries

You know we do like the story about the Japanese spokesman who told of the villagers of a certain place out west, who when an aeroplane came over ran up a perfect sea of neutral flags which nonplussed the aviator, who refrained from giving them the works and flew back home.

A correspondent asked what flags they were.

The spokesman replied that he could not do that, but could tell them the colours.

They were red, white and blue.

Of course, the dear chap must have his little joke!

* * *

Far Eastern Dictionary

Latest revised edition

ATTACK:—Standing in the way of a moving force. (See Defence *sub*)

CAUSE:—The effect of any action (See Effect *sub*)

CO-OPERATION:—The situation when one nation issues orders and the receiving nation obeys them instantly.

CULTURAL ADVANCEMENT:—The process of destroying institutions of higher learning, etc.

DEFENCE:—The act of blowing the daylights out of people hundreds of miles away from one's national boundaries. (See Attack *supra*)

ECONOMIC DEVELOPMENT:—The process of destroying cities, factories, railways, shopping, fishing junks and productive capacity generally.

EFFECT:—The cause of any action (See Cause *supra*)

FRIENDSHIP:—An emotion expressed by machine-gunning persons desired as friends.

GOOD NEIGHBOUR:—One who destroys the homes of those who live near by.

INSINCERITY:—Hesitation by one nation to carry out the orders issued to it by another nation.

* * *

Fifty-Fifty

General Matsui is reported to have declared that the Nine Power Conference is quite unnecessary. So, might we add, is all this back-chat going on round Shanghai.

* * *

The Coming Diplomacy

From a general survey of the international situation the new motto to be adopted by quite a large number of countries appears to be:—

"If you don't do what we want you to,
You'll get a swift kick in the slats."

* * *

The Question Why?

"But why," asks Prof. Herbert S. Liang, speaking before the Y's Men's Club, "are we so anti-Japanese? Why are we not anti-American, or anti-British, or anti-Russian?"

Dear, dear, dear! What short memories some of us seem to have!

* * *

Quite Natural

"Despite the rain," the communique said, "the soldiers are in 'very high spirits.'"

We try to keep the rain as much as possible out of our spirits too.

www.ingramcontent.com/pod-product-compliance
Lightning Source LLC
LaVergne TN
LVHW080353070526
838199LV00059B/3804